SCROLLS & STONES

Compelling Evidence the Bible Can Be Trusted

"Charlie Campbell's books and materials are incredible—beautifully illustrated, thoroughly researched, and very well written. He is an apologist extraordinaire! Don't miss his stuff—it will stretch your mind, stir your soul, and bless your heart."

–Dr. Ed Hindson
Distinguished Professor of Religion
at Liberty University

SCROLLS & STONES

Compelling Evidence the Bible Can Be Trusted

CHARLIE H. CAMPBELL

For my kids
and all those who desire to be ready
to give reasons for the hope they
have (1 Peter 3:15)

With thanks to Anastasia
and Rob Nash for their suggestions
on the manuscript

SCROLLS & STONES
Compelling Evidence the Bible Can Be Trusted

CONTENTS

INTRODUCTION

I believe God exists. And I believe very compelling, intellectually rigorous arguments can be made for His existence. The fine-tuning of the universe, the complexity of living cells, the information encoded into DNA, and other evidences from cosmology, biology, philosophy, history, and experience have led myself and millions of others to conclude that an incredibly intelligent, immensely powerful deity surely exists.[1] In addition to these evidences, I believe this deity, this God, has revealed Himself to humanity in and through the sixty-six books making up the Bible.

I don't know what your thoughts are about the Bible, but I hope you would agree with me that any book that claims to tell the truth about God and ends up being the best-selling, most

---

1. I discuss some of these evidences in my article "Evidence for the Existence of God" at AlwaysBeReady.com. Click on "God, Evidence for."

quoted, most published, most circulated, most translated,[2] most influential book in the history of mankind[3]—with no close second—is worth serious consideration. And yet, many people don't look into the Bible.

Of course, there are a variety of reasons for their disinterest, but many of them have doubts and questions about the Bible—good questions:

- How can we know the Bible isn't just an ancient book of fiction, folklore, or cleverly devised tales invented by deceitful men?
- Haven't books of the Bible been lost or tampered with down through the centuries?
- Isn't the Bible out-of-sync with scientific discoveries?
- Aren't there contradictions in the Bible?
- Why were certain books that mentioned Jesus left out of the New Testament?
- What makes the Bible any different than other religious books like the Quran or the Book of Mormon?

Those are questions people are asking today when the Bible comes up in conversation. And they have a right to ask those questions. Well, in this book, I'd like to try to answer them. I'll do this by laying out ten different lines of evidence for the trustworthiness of the Bible. We'll consider fulfilled prophecies,

----

2. United Bible Societies report that parts or all of the Bible have been translated into more than 2000 languages.

3. Norman Geisler and William Nix, *From God to Us: How We Got Our Bible* (2012), 11.

archaeological discoveries, scientific findings, ancient texts that corroborate people, places, and events in the Bible, and much more.

Of course, there are numerous, thick, scholarly books that address these issues and explore these kinds of evidences—many of them three hundred pages or more in length. But, for the sake of busy people who don't have time to read the heavy academic books on this subject, I will purposely keep this book much more concise. For those of you who want to learn more, I'll recommend some excellent resources along the way.

I think by the end of the book, as short as I intend to keep it, you'll see there are a wealth of good reasons why millions of people have concluded the Bible truly is the trustworthy Word of God (2 Timothy 3:16–17[4])—written by men, yes—but men who were guided by God as they penned its words (2 Peter 1:21[5]).

Charlie Campbell
March 29, 2014
Carlsbad, California

---

4. 2 Timothy 3:16–17 says, "All Scripture is inspired by God and profitable for teaching, for reproof, for correction, for training in righteousness; so that the man of God may be adequate, equipped for every good work."

5. 2 Peter 1:21 says, "For no prophecy was ever made by an act of human will, but men moved by the Holy Spirit spoke from God."

Evidence No. 1
FULFILLED PROPHECY
Spelled out in Advance

Humans have long been fascinated with trying to figure out the future. I understand the curiosity people have, for as someone once pointed out, "The future is where we will be spending the rest of our lives." Cashing in on that interest, every year astrologers, psychics, and prognosticators of a variety of stripes make their predictions as to what they think will happen in the coming year. At the beginning of 2013 some of the popular psychics' predictions included:

- A nuclear attack on New York City
- A huge earthquake in the Caribbean
- A chemical attack on the United States
- Experimental monkeys escaping from a lab causing a pandemic
- Apple releasing a "mini iPhone" geared toward children

Well, needless to say, these and dozens of other predictions by some of the most esteemed fortune-tellers failed to material-ize. Of course, a few of their predictions were correct. When it comes to picking election outcomes or whether or not a baby will be a boy or a girl, it's not hard to occasionally be right. But when it comes to foretelling the future with any kind of specific-ity beyond a few months out, mankind's track record has been absolutely dismal—that is, with the exception of some men liv-ing long ago in the Middle East.

Two to three thousand years ago there were men who boldly foretold world events with amazing accuracy. They claimed to have heard from God—the One who was able to declare "the end from the beginning and from ancient times things which have not been done."[6] And thus, having what we might call "inside information" about the future, they made hundreds of clear, specific predictions about what lied ahead. And astonish-ingly, over and over again, the words they proclaimed came to pass—often hundreds of years later.

These prophets' names were Moses, David, Isaiah, Jeremiah, Ezekiel, and Daniel, to name a few. They are the men whose

---

6. Isaiah 46:10.

teachings and proclamations are preserved for us in the pages of the Bible.

Their fulfilled prophecies are compelling evidence they had the help, the empowering, the supernatural aid of the One they claimed they were speaking for—the all-knowing, all-powerful creator of the universe, the One who could say, "Truly I have spoken; truly I will bring it to pass" (Isaiah 46:11). Knowing He alone had this capability, the God of the Bible challenged anyone else to:

> Declare to us what is going to take place…announce to us what is coming. Declare the things that are going to come afterward, that we may know that you are gods (Isaiah 41:22–23).

The God who laid out that challenge has never had any successful challengers. Fulfilled prophecy is something that sets the Bible apart from every other religious book. There are no fulfilled prophecies in the Hindu Vedas, the Quran, the Book of Mormon, or any other sacred religious writings. Not one.[7]

In stark contrast to these other writings, the Bible is literally filled with hundreds of specific, detailed prophecies that were made long before their fulfillment. In fact, 27% of the Bible contains what was predictive prophecy at the time it was written.[8] And Biblical prophets did not just predict some vague things

----

7. I have studied these writings and have come up completely empty-handed. If you think I've overlooked something, please email me some examples.

8. J. Barton Payne, *Encyclopedia of Biblical Prophecy* (1973), 681.

like Nostradamus[9] or Jeane Dixon (who have both proven to have been false prophets over and over again[10]), Biblical prophecies were very specific. Consider a few of the prophecies made regarding the Savior who God promised would come to redeem mankind:

- The Old Testament prophesied He would be a descendant of Abraham (Genesis 12:1–3, 22:18), Judah (Genesis 49:10), and David (2 Samuel 7:12f)
- Micah 5:2, written about 700 BC, said He would be born in the little town of Bethlehem
- Isaiah 7:14 said He would be born of a virgin (see Matthew 1:22–23)
- Malachi 3:1 declared He would come while the Jewish temple was still standing; the first century Jewish historian Flavius Josephus tells us Roman soldiers destroyed the temple in AD 70[11]
- Isaiah 35:5–6 foretold the kinds of miracles He would perform—opening the eyes of the blind, unstopping the ears of the deaf, and causing the lame to walk
- Isaiah 53:3 prophesied He would be "despised and forsaken"; Psalm 118:22 said He would be rejected by His own people (see 1 Peter 2:7)
- Daniel 9:24–26 foretold the precise time in history when

....

9. See a list of his predictions in Norman Geisler, "Nostradamus," *Baker Encyclopedia of Apologetics* (1999), 544–546.

10. See documentation of false predictions at ibid., 477, 544–546.

11. Flavius Josephus, *The Wars of the Jews*, Books 6 and 7.

He would die; it says He would be "cut off" (murdered) before the people (the Romans) would "destroy the city [Jerusalem] and the sanctuary [the temple]"[12]

- Psalm 22:16–18, written by David about 1000 BC and three to four hundred years before the art of crucifixion was invented,[13] told us His hands and feet would be pierced during His death; Isaiah 53 and Zechariah 12 provide even more details surrounding His death
- Psalm 16:10 and Isaiah 53:10 prophesied He would rise from the dead (see Acts 2:27–32)

Of course, all those prophecies and many more[14] were fulfilled in the life of one person, Jesus Christ. Oxford University scholar H. P. Liddon noted that the Old Testament has 332 distinct predictions that were literally fulfilled in Jesus's life[15] (see note below about the use of *Jesus's* instead of *Jesus*"[16]).

Computations using the science of probability on just eight of these prophecies show the chance that someone could have fulfilled all eight prophecies is one in 10^{17} or 1 in 100

....

12. See a good Bible commentary for help unpacking this incredible prophecy.

13. "Crucifixion," *The Encyclopedia Britannica* (2013), http://www.britannica.com/EB-checked/topic/144583/crucifixion.

14. There is a much longer list of prophecies Jesus fulfilled at AlwaysBeReady.com.

15. Robert Saucy, "Scripture" in Chuck Swindoll and Roy Zuck (eds.), *Understanding Christian Theology* (2003), 44.

16. *The Chicago Manual of Style* now recommends that Biblical and classical names form the possessive with both an apostrophe and "s," even if they already end in "s." Among the examples given are "Jesus's adherents" and "Tacitus's *Histories*."

quadrillion.[17]

SKEPTIC: "Now, hold on a second Charlie. Maybe the early Christians just made up all the things Jesus supposedly did. Perhaps they read all those prophecies in the Old Testament and decided to make up an elaborate story about Jesus fulfilling them!"

Well, I'm not sure what their motivation would have been for doing that. Liars lie to get out of trouble or gain some type of advantage or benefit. But what the early Christians said about Jesus, didn't get them *out* of trouble or result in any kind of benefit. The words they said and wrote about Jesus got them *in* trouble. What they received was "rejection, persecution, torture, and martyrdom. Hardly a list of perks!"[18] I'll talk more about this in chapter eight.

In addition to prophecies about Jesus, there are lots of other prophecies in the Bible about a variety of matters surrounding the rise and fall of nations,[19] the regathering of the Jewish people back into their homeland[20] (something that's being fulfilled right now), and much more. The fact that these and hundreds of other prophecies have been fulfilled, even though they were

....

17. Peter Stoner, former Chairman of the Departments of Mathematics and Astronomy at Pasadena City College and an expert in mathematical probabilities, discusses his peer-reviewed calculations in his book *Science Speaks*. His book is available online for free and the particular chapter containing his calculations regarding Jesus can be found here: http://sciencespeaks.dstoner.net/Christ_of_Prophecy.html#c9. The concise wording I use above comes from Fritz Ridenour, *So What's the Difference?* (2001), 28.

18. Peter Kreeft, in Norman Geisler and Paul Hoffman (eds.), *Why I am a Christian: Leading Thinkers Explain Why They Believe* (2006), 250.

19. Edom, Philistia, Egypt, Babylonia, Persia, Assyria, Greece, Ethiopia, Moab, Ammon, Syria and other nations and cities are addressed in Biblical prophecies. See John Walvoord's excellent book *Every Prophecy of the Bible*.

20. For example, see Ezekiel 36–39.

made centuries before their fulfillment, is strong evidence that Biblical prophets spoke with the authority and foresight of the all-knowing, all-powerful God they claimed to be speaking for.

For a more in-depth examination of fulfilled prophecies in the Bible, I recommend:

- *Every Prophecy of the Bible* by John Walvoord
- *Encyclopedia of Biblical Prophecy* by J. Barton Payne
- *Handbook of Biblical Evidences* by John Ankerberg and John Weldon

Evidence No. 2
ARCHAEOLOGICAL DISCOVERIES
Stones that Cry Out

Recently, I was flying to Florida to give a series of talks on the reliability of the Bible when a gentleman in his fifties named Randy sat down next to me. He had graciously given up a different seat to allow a husband and wife to sit next to each other. As this well-dressed businessman from Denver was getting settled into his new seat, he asked me why I was flying. I told him I was headed to Tampa to do some teaching on the Bible. He rolled his eyes and chuckled a bit as though that would be a huge waste of time. He explained that he had long ago concluded the Bible was a "book of myths." I asked how he came to that conclusion and he confidently proclaimed, "There is no archaeological evidence to support it."

I had to bite my lip to keep from chuckling myself. Here I was, hours away from giving three different talks on evidence for the Bible—including a 50 minute presentation on archaeological evidence—and this man tells me there is "no archaeological evidence to support it." I don't know if you believe God moves people around on planes for "divine appointments." I do. So, after offering up a quick thank you to God for rearranging this man's seat, I began to explain to Randy some of the reasons I had concluded the Bible *is* trustworthy—including the wealth of archaeological evidence.

I think Randy was a little surprised to find out his ill-founded "I read it in *The Da Vinci Code*" conclusions could be overthrown by an avalanche of facts and evidence that proved otherwise.

Of course, there are a lot of people out there like Randy. They've read a book like *The Da Vinci Code* or seen a YouTube video attacking the Bible and they've come to the conclusion that the Bible is a "book of myths," a compilation of folklore, legends, and "cleverly devised tales"[21] penned by deceitful men.

Well, they've arrived at these conclusions not realizing that thousands of archaeological discoveries over the past 150 years have verified the exact truthfulness of the Bible's detailed records of various events, customs, persons, cities, nations, and geographical locations.

Dr. Nelson Glueck, who appeared on the cover of *Time*

---

21. 2 Peter 1:16.

magazine and who has been credited with uncovering more than fifteen hundred ancient sites in the Middle East,[22] wrote:

> No archaeological discovery has ever controverted [overturned] a Biblical reference. Scores of archaeological findings have been made which confirm in clear outline or in exact detail historical statements in the Bible. And, by the same token, proper evaluation of Biblical descriptions has often led to amazing discoveries.[23]

James Mann of *U. S. News and World Report* said:

> A wave of archaeological discoveries is altering old ideas about the roots of Christianity and Judaism—and affirming that the Bible is more historically accurate than many scholars thought.[24]

Dr. Clifford Wilson, the former Director of the Australian Institute of Archaeology, stated:

> It is remarkable that where confirmation is possible and has come to light, the Bible stands investigation in ways that are unique in all literature. Its superiority to attack, its capac-

22. "Archaeology: The Shards of History," *Time* magazine, December 13, 1963. No author named.

23. Nelson Glueck, *Rivers in the Desert* (1968), 31.

24. James Mann, "New Finds Cast Fresh Light on the Bible," *U. S. News and World Report*, August 24, 1981, 34.

ity to withstand criticism, its amazing facility to be proved right after all, are all staggering by any standards of scholarship. Seemingly assured results "disproving" the Bible have a habit of backfiring. Over and over again the Bible has been vindicated.[25]

Allow me to share a few examples of discoveries that have helped to shed light on the Bible's reliability.

Until 1993, not a shred of evidence could be found anywhere outside the Bible that David, the king of Israel, ever existed and so it had become fashionable in some academic circles to dismiss the David stories as mere invention. The critics' verdict was that David was "nothing more than a figure of religious and political mythology."[26]

Well, their skepticism regarding David collapsed overnight in 1993 when a nearly 3000-year-old inscription was unearthed in Israel mentioning David the king of Israel. This was a tremendous discovery and helped to verify for the first time outside the Bible that David was an actual historical figure. In light of this discovery, *Time* magazine stated, "The skeptics' claim that King David never existed is now hard to defend."[27] Indeed it is. And it has gotten even harder now that a second reference to David

....

25. Clifford Wilson, *Archaeology—the Bible and Christ*, volume 17, (Victoria, Australia: Pacific Christian Ministries), no page number available. Cited in John Ankerberg and John Weldon, *Handbook of Biblical Evidences* (1997), 288–289.

26. Jeffrey Sheler, *Is the Bible True?* (1999), 95–96.

27. Michael D. Lemonick, "Are the Bible's Stories True? Archaeology's Evidence," *Time* magazine, December 18, 1995, http://www.time.com/time/magazine/article/0,9171,983854-6,00.html.

has been identified on the ancient "Moabite Stone" discovered in Jordan—now on display at the Louvre in Paris.[28]

Completely overlooking these discoveries, the outspoken atheist Richard Dawkins gave his *God Delusion* readers the impression David might be a myth by attaching the phrase "if he existed"[29] to his name. Well, Mr. Dawkins is either woefully behind in his reading for someone who speaks so passionately about these matters or he's happy to just overlook archaeological discoveries that stand firmly in the way of his agenda.

Another fascinating discovery concerns Pontius Pilate. The New Testament authors tell us he was the Roman governor of Judea at the time of Jesus who oversaw His trial and then sentenced Him to death by crucifixion (Matthew 27:2; Luke 3:1). Was Pilate a legendary figure? No.

In 1961, a team of Italian archaeologists was digging in Caesarea, on the shore of the beautiful Mediterranean Sea in Israel. While clearing away the sand and overgrowth from the jumbled ruins of a Roman theater, these archaeologists made an astonishing find. They uncovered a limestone block that bore an inscription in Latin dating to the early part of the first century that mentioned "Pontius Pilate, Prefect of Judea."

This inscription verifies that Pontius Pilate was an actual historical person, that he reigned in the very position ascribed to him by the Gospels, and as prefect he would have had the authority to condemn or pardon Jesus, just as the Gospel

....

28. Kenneth Kitchen discusses this in his book *On the Reliability of the Old Testament* (2003), 92–93. Also see James Hoffmeier, *The Archaeology of the Bible* (2008), 87–88.

29. Richard Dawkins, *The God Delusion* (2006), 93.

accounts report. Since the time of this discovery, Pilate's official residence at Caesarea has also been identified.

Another discovery helped to verify the reality of crucifixion in Israel in the first century. According to the Bible, Jesus's hands or wrists were nailed to the cross (John 20:25). But at one time, critics said crucifixions with nails never took place in Israel in the first century. No evidence of any crucified victim had ever been uncovered in Israel—so skeptics and scholars dismissed the Gospels' accounts as either imagined or inaccurate.[30]

Well, critics of the Bible were shown to be wrong again in 1968. It was then that a crew of builders from the Israel Ministry of Housing working in Jerusalem accidentally discovered an ancient Jewish cemetery that contained the remains of several men who were killed during the Jewish revolt against Rome in approximately AD 70. One of the bone ossuaries contained the skeleton of a young man and an inscription of the man's name (Yohanan Ben Ha'galgol). What stunned the archaeologists most though was how this man died. He was put to death by crucifixion with nails. How was that determined? He still had an iron spike driven through his heel bone. The Romans typically removed the nails from their victims—iron was expensive—but apparently this nail was too difficult to remove. The tip of the nail had been bent back toward the head, likely the result of hitting a knot in the wood. And so, the soldiers left it there. And now we have solid archaeological evidence that the Romans *did* crucify people in Israel, in the first century, with nails—just as

....

30. Randall Price, "Archaeology and the Bible," http://www.worldofthe bible.com/resources.htm.

the Bible said.

Other discoveries include:

- **Ancient extrabiblical accounts of a catastrophic flood** (Genesis 6–8)[31]
- **The palace of Sennacherib** the king of Assyria (2 Chronicles 32:1f) and a wall relief depicting the Assyrian siege on Lachish (2 Kings 18:13–17; Isaiah 36:1–2)
- **The ruins of Jericho** (Joshua 6) along with evidence the city wall "fell down flat" (6:20) at the very time the Old Testament dates the crossing of the Hebrew people into Canaan (c. 1400 BC)[32]
- **Hezekiah's tunnel** (2 Kings 20:20) built to secretly channel water into the city of Jerusalem c. 700 BC
- **The ancient ruins of Babylon** (Book of Daniel), including the ruins of king Nebuchadnezzar's palaces, temples, city walls, houses, inscriptions mentioning "Nebuchadnezzar, King of Babylon"
- **The Babylonian Chronicle tablets** that mention the siege against Jerusalem (2 Kings 24) and that the Babylonians took the Jews captive back to Babylon just as the Bible said (Daniel 1)
- **The "Pool of Siloam"** (John 9:1–12) where Jesus sent the

31. I discuss this more in chapter 4.

32. Michael D. Lemonick and Katherine L. Mihok, "Score One for the Bible," *Time* magazine, March 5, 1990, http://www.time.com/time/magazine/article/0,9171,969538,00.html. Also see: Bryant Wood, "The Walls of Jericho," June 9, 2008, http://www.biblearchaeology.org/post/2008/06/the-walls-of-jericho.aspx.

blind man with mud on his eyes to wash and receive
healing

- **The well called "Jacob's Well"** (John 4:6) where Jesus
met the Samaritan woman
- **The pool called "Bethesda"** (John 5:2) where Jesus told
the man who had been lame for 38 years to take up his
bed and walk
- **Herod's palace** (Mark 6:14–29) where John the Baptist
was imprisoned and killed; the historian Josephus mentions this palace and John the Baptist's imprisonment
and murder there[33]
- **A bone ossuary mentioning Caiaphas** the Jewish high
priest (Matthew 26:3) who presided over Jesus's late
night trial (Matthew 26:57–68)
- **The synagogue in Capernaum** (Mark 1:21) on the north
shore of the Sea of Galilee where Jesus often taught
- **Mosaic tile floor of an early Christian church** in
Megiddo, Israel, that says the church was built in the
memory of "the God Jesus Christ"—evidence the early
Christians believed Jesus was God[34]

Many more examples could be cited. My book *Archaeological Evidence for the Bible* discusses these and dozens of other
finds.[35] But friend, you can go to Israel, as I have, and see these

33. Flavius Josephus, *The Antiquities of the Jews*, Book 18, Chapter 5:2. I talk more about
this in chapter four.

34. I talk more about evidence for Jesus's existence in chapter four.

35. Available at AlwaysBeReady.com.

and hundreds of other discoveries with your own eyes. They are an incredible evidence of the Bible's trustworthiness.

Contrast this with what archaeology has *not* been able to do for the Book of Mormon. Archaeologists seeking to confirm the truthfulness of events spoken about in the Book of Mormon have come up completely empty-handed. Mormon archaeologist Dee Green, who was formerly the editor of the *University Archaeological Society Newsletter*, published at Brigham Young University, said:

> No Book of Mormon location is known with reference to modern topography. Biblical archaeology can be studied because we do know where Jerusalem and Jericho were and are, but we do not know where Zarahemla and Bountiful[36] (nor any other location for that matter) were or are. It would seem then that a concentration on geography should be the first order of business, but we have already seen that twenty years of such an approach has left us *empty-handed*.[37]

The National Geographic Society and the Smithsonian Institute have confirmed this as well with statements in 1996 and 1998.[38]

Dave Hunt, an expert on religions and cults, summarized the results:

....

36. Places spoken of in the Book of Mormon.

37. *Dialogue: A Journal of Mormon Thought* (Summer 1969), 77–78. Italics added.

38. You can look at photocopies of their statements regarding the Book of Mormon at AlwaysBeReady.com. Click on "Mormonism."

Not one piece of evidence has ever been found to support the Book of Mormon—not a trace of the large cities it names, no ruins, no coins, no letters or documents or monuments, nothing in writing. Not even one of the rivers or mountains or any of the topography it mentions has ever been identified![39]

Friend, nothing has ever been found which demonstrates the Book of Mormon is anything other than an early nineteenth century piece of American fiction, invented by Joseph Smith.[40]

If you would like to learn more about archaeological discoveries that have helped to confirm the Bible, I recommend:

- *The Popular Handbook of Archaeology and the Bible* by Joseph Holden and Norman Geisler
- *Archaeology and the New Testament* by John McRay
- *Archaeology and the Old Testament* by Alfred Hoerth
- *The Archaeology of the Bible* by James Hoffmeier
- *The Stones Cry Out* by Randall Price

39. Dave Hunt, *In Defense of the Faith* (2009), 164. Also see Lee Strobel, *The Case for Christ* (1998), 107.

40. I address numerous other problems with the Book of Mormon at AlwaysBeReady. com. Click on "Mormonism."

Evidence No. 3
INTERNAL CONSISTENCY
Structurally Harmonious

A third line of evidence the Bible is what it claims to be is its internal consistency. I am talking about the Bible's internal harmony. From the first book of the Bible (Genesis) to the last book (Revelation), the Bible is absolutely consistent in what it teaches.

SKEPTIC: "Why is that an evidence of divine origin? There are plenty of books that are internally consistent!"

I agree. Back in the 1990s I worked for a surfing magazine a block from the ocean in downtown Laguna Beach, California. It was a surfer's dream job. We put out an internally consistent magazine every month. Does that mean the authors of our different articles were writing down God-inspired Scripture? No. I can assure you of that! Then what makes the Bible any different than some other book or magazine that is internally consistent? There are a variety of reasons I believe the internal consistency of the Bible is an amazing evidence of its divine origin.

A. The Bible addresses life's most controversial questions.

At the surfing magazine we wrote about who won the latest surf contest, surf wax, sunscreen—pretty trivial matters looking back on it all now (though I loved my job and still love the people I worked with!). But these were not the type of matters the authors of the Bible addressed. No. They tackled the big questions of life:

- How did the universe come into existence?
- Does God exist? If so, what is He like?
- Why do people exist?
- What is our purpose for being here?
- Why is there evil and suffering in the world?
- What happens to us after we die?
- What is God's plan for humanity?

These are the big controversial questions of life. These are the kinds of questions people tend to disagree about—just ask your neighbors!—and yet, they are the very questions the authors of the Bible tackle head on, chapter after chapter, book after book, from beginning to end. And they do so absolutely consistently.

B. The Bible is a collection of 66 different documents.

We might expect to find the Bible internally consistent if the Bible was a single book, but it's not. It's a compilation of more than five-dozen different books.

C. The Bible was written by approximately 40 different authors.

In contrast to the Bible, the Quran is a single book containing the teachings of just one man—Muhammad (AD 570–632).

We would expect it to be internally harmonious. It's not. It has numerous contradictory statements in it.[41] The fact that the Bible contains the teachings, the writings, of approximately 40 different people and yet remains internally consistent is astounding.

D. Many of the Bible's authors came from different educational and cultural backgrounds.

Moses was a prince in Egypt who was raised and "educated in all the learning of the Egyptians" (Acts 7:22) before becoming a shepherd. Joshua was a soldier. David was a shepherd, then a king. Asaph, a musician. Daniel, a government official in Babylon. Ezra, a scribe. Nehemiah, a cupbearer for King Artaxerxes Longimanus in Shushan, in western Iran. Peter, a fisherman. Paul, a scholar from Tarsus in the southeast of Asia Minor. Matthew, a tax collector for the Roman government. Luke, a Gentile physician. It's not difficult to see why one might expect their writings to be a rat's nest of contradictory views.

E. The Bible was written over a period of approximately 1500 years.

Many of the authors did not even know one another; they were separated by hundreds of years in time.

F. Many of the authors were separated by hundreds of miles geographically.

....

41. See "Contradictions in the Quran," http://www.answering-islam.org/Quran/Contra/index.html.

The Bible was written in a variety of places on three different continents—Africa, Asia, and Europe. For example, Moses wrote in the wilderness of the Sinai Peninsula. Paul wrote four letters imprisoned in Rome. The apostle John wrote the Book of Revelation while a prisoner banished to the Isle of Patmos in the Mediterranean Sea. The prophet Ezekiel wrote his work while held captive in Babylon.

G. The Bible was written in three different languages: Hebrew, Aramaic, and Greek.

Now, I don't know about you, but when I think of pulling together forty different people (spread out over fifteen centuries, on three different continents, who speak three different languages) to write sixty-six different documents regarding life's most controversial questions—I'm thinking we are going to have some serious problems. That book is a going to be a confusing and difficult read!

Yet, in spite of all these factors, the Bible is a perfectly harmonious, consistent account of how God is seeking to reconcile sinners like you and me back into relationship with Himself.

This internal consistency is powerful evidence the authors of the Bible were being guided by the Holy Spirit when they wrote the different books of the Bible (2 Timothy 3:16; 2 Peter 1:21).

SKEPTIC: "Charlie, how can you say this—that the Bible is internally consistent? The Bible has numerous contradictions!"

Ah, the alleged contradictions in the Bible. There are some verses in the Bible that can seem out-of-sync with other verses.

But with a little investigation into the context of the various passages, the cultural and geographical settings the Bible was originally written in, and occasionally the original languages, they are easily explained. Allow me to walk you through a couple apparent contradictions and show you how they can be resolved. If you'd like to look at more of these, go to AlwaysBeReady.com and click on "Bible Difficulties."

The first one we'll consider has to do with the number of angels at Jesus's tomb. Notice what Matthew 28:2–7 says (italics added):

> And behold, a severe earthquake had occurred, for *an angel* of the Lord descended from heaven and came and rolled away the stone and sat upon it. And his appearance was like lightning, and his clothing as white as snow. The guards shook for fear of him and became like dead men. *The angel* said to the women, "Do not be afraid; for I know that you are looking for Jesus who has been crucified. He is not here, for He has risen, just as He said. Come, see the place where He was lying. Go quickly and tell His disciples that He has risen from the dead; and behold, He is going ahead of you into Galilee, there you will see Him; behold, I have told you."

It appears from what Matthew wrote that there was only one angel at the tomb at the time of Jesus's resurrection.

Now, John chapter 20 seems to say something that contradicts this—well, at least the critics think so. Notice what John 20:11–12 says (italics added):

But Mary was standing outside the tomb weeping; and so, as she wept, she stooped and looked into the tomb; and she saw *two angels* in white sitting, one at the head and one at the feet, where the body of Jesus had been lying.

John makes it clear that Mary saw two angels. So, the critic says, "Ha! Look at that! Matthew says there was one angel on the scene and John says there were two! Contradiction!"

Is this really a contradiction as critics suppose? Not at all. First off, notice verse 10. It says, "So the disciples went away again to their own homes." Notice that. John indicates the disciples (with the exception of Mary) had already visited the empty grave and *gone home*. This is something critics almost always fail to notice. And that's unfortunate, because knowing that verses 11 and 12 take place *later* in the day helps solve the alleged problem.

Let's suppose you email a friend and say, "I saw *a* pastor at church today." Now, someone else comes along after you and emails that same person and says, "I saw *two* pastors at church today." Has this person contradicted your previous statement? Not at all. This person is just giving a fuller account of what happened. He's making it clear there was actually more than one pastor on the scene. It's not that you were wrong when you said you saw "a pastor." You were just speaking with a narrower view of the day's events.

The same is true with the accounts of the angels at Jesus's tomb. Matthew mentioned one angel—the angel who rolled away the stone in Matthew 28. John, talking about a scene later in the morning, tells us there were two angels on the scene. The accounts are not contradictory. They are complementary. The solution is so simple, it's hard to believe this is so often cited as a contradiction.

One of the mistakes critics of the Bible commonly make is *assuming a partial report is a false report.*[42] There are places in the Bible, especially in the Gospels, where one author chose to leave out certain details in his account of an event that another author chose to include. The critic comes along, reads both passages, and then assumes one of the authors has erred or contradicted the other writer. But this is an error on the part of the critic. It is perfectly acceptable—even in today's society—for reporters and biographers who are writing about the same event or person, to include or omit details others do not. When we read the news on two different websites, we *expect* to read some different details about the same story. If the Gospels all included the exact same details with similar wording, they would have been discredited long ago on grounds of collusion.

Another popular "contradiction" concerns Jesus's occupation. Notice what Mark 6:2–3 says (italics added):

When the Sabbath came, He [Jesus] began to teach in the synagogue; and the many listeners were astonished, saying, "Where did this man get these things, and what is this wisdom given to Him, and such miracles as these performed by His hands? Is not this the *carpenter*, the son of Mary, and

42. Norman Geisler and Thomas Howe have a list of 17 mistakes critics make when reading the Bible in *The Big Book of Bible Difficulties* (2008), 15–26.

brother of James and Joses and Judas and Simon? Are not His sisters here with us?" And they took offense at Him.

According to this passage, we learn that Jesus was a carpenter. Now, notice what Matthew 13:54–55 says (italics added):

> He [Jesus] came to His hometown and began teaching them in their synagogue, so that they were astonished, and said, "Where did this man get this wisdom and these miraculous powers? Is not this the *carpenter's son?*"

Critics, on the lookout for ways to discredit the Bible, say the Gospels contradict one another here. Why? Well, one says *Jesus* was a carpenter (Mark 6:3) and another says His *father* was the carpenter (Matthew 13:55).

What's the solution? Was Jesus the carpenter as Mark tells us? Or was Joseph the carpenter as Matthew tells us? You don't need to be a rocket scientist to think this through. I've asked junior high kids this question. And almost all of them raise their hands eager to share the answer. They were *both* carpenters! Jesus, like most men at that time, followed in the footsteps of his father. The crowd of people knew that and were asking *both* questions: "Is not this the carpenter?" (Mark 6:3) and "Is not this the carpenter's son?" (Matthew 13:55). This apparent contradiction is laid to rest with some careful junior high level reflection (as is the case with many of them).

Critics of the Bible would be wise to consult a good Bible commentary or book on Bible difficulties before passing judgment on the Bible.[43] These kinds of solutions are readily available to the person willing to do a little homework.

SKEPTIC: "Charlie, even if you're able to demonstrate the entire Bible is free of these kinds of contradictions, it could all just be the result of Christians purposely leaving out the books that didn't agree with the Bible."

Christians in the early church of the first three centuries *did* leave some books out of the Bible. And there's a good reason why. They never belonged *in* the Bible!

When the so-called *Gospel of Thomas* and other "gospels" purportedly written by Judas, Philip, and Mary Magdalene started appearing on the scene long after these persons had died, Christians recognized them for what they were—pseudo gospels that were uninspired, spurious writings. They realized these writings were not written by Thomas and the others, but by false teachers seeking to influence the Christian church with their unbiblical ideas. Scholars, Christian and non-Christian, date these "gospels" to the second and third centuries—long after the time Jesus, Judas, Thomas, Mary Magdalene, and Philip lived.[44]

In addition to the late arrival of these writings, there was plenty of internal evidence that gave them away as fakes. Con-

....

43. A couple commentaries I recommend are: *The Bible Knowledge Commentary* edited by John Walvoord and Roy Zuck and *The MacArthur Bible Commentary* by John MacArthur. For books specifically addressing Bible difficulties, I recommend *The Big Book of Bible Difficulties* by Norman Geisler and Thomas Howe and *Commonly Misunderstood Bible Verses* by Ron Rhodes.

44. Erwin Lutzer says, "Even scholars who want to give these documents credibility say that the very earliest date is about AD 150, at least one hundred or, more likely, one hundred and fifty years after the time of Jesus's crucifixion." *The Da Vinci Deception* (2004), 27.

sider these outlandish, even sexist words *The Gospel of Thomas* puts in the mouths of the apostle Peter and Jesus. Peter supposedly says to Jesus:

> "Make Mary leave us, for females don't deserve life." Jesus said, "Look, I will guide her to make her male, so that she too may become a living spirit resembling you males. For every female who makes herself male will enter the domain of Heaven."[45]

I think you can see why the early Christians knew instantly that this was nothing Peter or Jesus would have said.

Consider the so-called *Gospel of Judas*.[46] Some of the bizarre things put forth in it include:

- Judas telling Jesus that He was "from the immortal realm of Barbelo"[47]
- Jesus telling Judas that he (Judas) will be "cursed by ...other generations" for his deeds only to one day "rule over them"[48]
- Jesus honoring Judas above the other disciples by giving him privileged information about "the mysteries of the

45. *The Gospel of Thomas*, 114.

46. Available online here: http://www.nationalgeographic.com/lostgospel/_pdf/GospelofJudas.pdf.

47. *The Gospel of Judas*, hardcover published by National Geographic (2006), 23.

48. Ibid., 33.

kingdom"[49]

- Judas being commended by Jesus for betraying Him into the hands of those who would crucify Him and liberate His spirit from His physical body (a deed that would exceed all other good deeds)[50]

Well, of course these and many other strange statements contradicted the *known* teachings of Jesus and the apostles regarding Judas (e.g., Matthew 26:24, 27:3–10; John 6:70–71). And so, it was immediately obvious to the early Christians (e.g., Irenaeus[51] and Tertullian[52]—two prominent church fathers who wrote about *The Gospel of Judas*) that this "gospel" was not genuine or trustworthy. And it was left out of the Bible.

Should the early Christians have accepted every fraudulent book (containing things they knew were not true) into the Bible to avoid the charge centuries later that "they purposely left out certain books"? I think not. Should editors of the *Encyclopedia Britannica* accept articles submitted to them, even if the articles contradict what they know to be true regarding a certain matter? Of course not. I'm glad they don't do that. And we can be thankful the early Christians didn't do that either.

New Testament scholar, Dr. Craig Evans tells his students who are curious about these writings outside the New Testa-

....

49. Ibid., 23.

50. Ibid., 43.

51. Irenaeus, *Against Heresies*, Book 1, Chapter 31. http://www.ccel.org/ccel/schaff/anf01.ix.ii.xxxii.html.

52. Tertullian, *Against All Heresies*, Chapter 2. http://www.ccel.org/ccel/schaff/anf03.v.xi.ii.html.

ment, to read them. He says, "You tell me: Should [*The Gospel of*] *Thomas* be right alongside Matthew, Mark, Luke, and John?" Without exception, after they read them, they come back and say, "My goodness, what weird stuff."[53] If you read them, I think you'll come to the same conclusion.

For more help understanding why certain non-Christian writings from the second and third centuries were left out of the Bible, see:

- *The Case for the Real Jesus* (2007) by Lee Strobel; see interview with Craig Evans, 23–63
- "Nag Hammadi Gospels" and "Gospel of Thomas" in *The Big Book of Christian Apologetics* by Norman Geisler
- *The Missing Gospels* by Darrell Bock
- *Judas and the Gospel of Jesus* by N. T. Wright
- "From Traitor to Hero? Responding to *The Gospel of Judas*" by Albert Mohler[54]

....

53. Lee Strobel, *The Case for the Real Jesus* (2007), 43.

54. Available online at www.albertmohler.com.

Evidence No. 4
EXTRABIBLICAL WRITINGS
Spoken About Outside the Bible

Read this short passage about John the Baptist. And then I have a question for you.

> John, that was called the Baptist…was a good man, and commanded the Jews to exercise virtue, both as to righteousness towards one another, and piety towards God, and so to come to baptism…Herod, who feared the great influence John had over the people…sent [John] a prisoner, out of Herod's suspicious temper, to Macherus, the castle I before mentioned, and was there put to death.

Who do you think wrote those words about John the Baptist? Matthew? No. Mark? Luke? John? Paul? No.

Though this passage reads like it was taken right out of the New Testament, it was actually written by the first century historian Flavius Josephus (AD 37/38–97).[55] And notice the passage again. He verifies for us that John the Baptist was an actual person and that he was put to death by Herod Antipas, just as the

---

55. Flavius Josephus, *The Antiquities of the Jews*, Book 18, Chapter 5:2.

Bible says (Matthew 14:1–10).

Many people don't realize there are dozens of writings that survive *outside* of the Bible in the records of the Assyrians, Babylonians, and Romans that verify the historical accuracy of the Bible's records of different persons, places, and events. These extrabiblical writings have helped corroborate the existence of fifty some persons mentioned in the Old Testament and more than thirty persons written about in the New Testament.[56]

They've also helped verify certain details surrounding Jesus's life. Now, unbelievably, some critics of Christianity today are telling people that Jesus never existed—that He was the invention of some clever deceivers in the first century. Of course, this claim is not new. The British philosopher, Bertrand Russell (1872–1970) wrote in his famous essay *Why I Am Not a Christian*, "Historically it is quite doubtful whether Christ ever existed at all, and if he did we do not know anything about Him."[57]

Well, the claim "Jesus never existed" is absurd and only demonstrates the critics' ignorance of the facts or perhaps their willingness to overlook the facts. Why? Because there is very good historical evidence *outside* of the Bible that Jesus lived. More than thirty extrabiblical sources mention Him within 150 years of His life. And they don't just mention Him, they corroborate numerous details spoken about Him in the New

....

56. See Joseph Holden and Norman Geisler, *The Popular Handbook of Archaeology and the Bible* (2013), 283–289 for OT persons; 303–305 for NT persons.

57. Bertrand Russell, *Why I Am Not A Christian: And Other Essays on Religion and Related Subjects* (1957), 16.

Testament.[58]

One of these external sources is Josephus. In his writings, he mentions more than a dozen individuals talked about in the Bible, including: Herod the Great, Herod Antipas, Caiaphas, Pontius Pilate, John the Baptist, James "the brother of Jesus, called Christ," Felix, and Festus. Here is one excerpt where he mentions Jesus:

> At this time there was a wise man who was called Jesus. And his conduct was good and was known to be virtuous. And many people from among the Jews and the other nations became his disciples. Pilate condemned him to be crucified to die. And those who had become his disciples did not abandon his discipleship. They reported that he had appeared to them three days after his crucifixion and that he was alive; accordingly, he was perhaps the Messiah concerning whom the prophets have recounted wonders.[59]

Notice that. Not only does Josephus mention Jesus, he tells us that Jesus was known to be a good and virtuous person, He was crucified under the reign of Pontius Pilate, and His disciples reported that He rose from the grave.

....

58. Gary Habermas documents these sources and comments on them in his book *The Historical Jesus: Ancient Evidence for the Life of Christ*. Also see Norman Geisler, *Baker Encyclopedia of Apologetics* (1999), 381–385; F. F. Bruce, *Jesus and Christian Origins Outside the New Testament*.

59. I have purposely taken this quote from a surviving Arabic version of Josephus's writings cited by Gary Habermas in his *Historical Jesus* (1996), 192–196. The Arabic version is considered by some to be more reliable than the wording that survives in other languages. See Josephus, *Antiquities of the Jews*, Book 18, Chapter 3:3.

Now, some critics of the Bible say this quote by Josephus must have been forged by Christians who came along after Josephus and tampered with his writings. Well, there's no evidence this ever occurred. Eusebius (c. 260–340 AD), the early church historian, quotes Josephus's words with only minuscule insignificant differences when compared with the text that survives today.[60] So, if any tampering took place, it must have occurred *before* then. But why would Christians living before Eusebius even want to insert a paragraph about Jesus into Josephus's writings? There was no debate going on regarding Jesus's existence in those early centuries. I agree with Dr. Gary Habermas, author of *The Historical Jesus: Ancient Evidence for the Life of Christ*, who says:

> There are good indications that the majority of the text is genuine. There is no textual evidence against it, and, conversely, there is very good manuscript evidence for this statement about Jesus...Additionally, leading scholars on the works of Josephus have testified that this portion is written in the style of this Jewish historian.[61]

But even if we were to lay this quote aside, this is not the only place where Josephus mentioned Jesus. He mentioned Him

---

60. Eusebius, *Ecclesiastical History*, Book 1, Chapter 11:7.
61. Gary Habermas, *The Historical Jesus* (1999), 193.

elsewhere.[62] But even if all of Josephus's writings were tampered with, there is still an abundance of evidence Jesus was a real person.

Take for example, the Jewish Talmud. The Talmud is a compilation of Jewish teachings that were passed down from generation to generation amongst the Jews and then finally compiled and organized after the destruction of Jerusalem in AD 70. Here is an excerpt that mentions Jesus:

On the eve of Passover, Yeshu [a Hebrew word referring to Jesus[63]] was hanged. For forty days before the execution took place, a herald went forth and cried, "He is going forth to be stoned because he has practiced sorcery and enticed Israel to apostasy. Any one who can say anything in his favor, let him come forward and plead on his behalf." But since nothing was brought forward in his favor he was hanged on the eve of the Passover![64]

So, note that. Not only does the Talmud mention Jesus, it mentions His crucifixion and the Jewish leadership's desire to stone Jesus (compare with John 8:58–59, 10:31–33, 39). And notice

....

62. In *Antiquities of the Jews*, Book 20, Chapter 9:1, Josephus wrote of the Sanhedrin who "brought before them the brother of Jesus, who was called Christ, whose name was James." Dr. Walter C. Kaiser points out that such a passing reference to Jesus suggests either Josephus felt Jesus needed no introduction or Josephus himself had already introduced Him to the reader in Book 18, Chapter 3:63–64. *Archaeological Study Bible* (2005), 1751.

63. *Yeshu* is "Joshua" in Hebrew; the Greek equivalent is translated as Jesus. See a discussion of this in Lee Strobel's *The Case for the Real Jesus* (2007), 113.

64. Babylonian Talmud, Sanhedrin 43a.

that it even says Jesus was put to death at the time of the Passover—the very time the New Testament says the crucifixion occurred (John 18:28)!

Other sources that mention Jesus outside of the Bible include the Roman historian Cornelius Tacitus (c. AD 55–120), Gaius Suetonius (AD 69–died after 122) the chief secretary of the Roman Emperor Hadrian (who reigned AD 117–138), and Pliny the Younger (AD 61/62–c. 113) a Roman author and administrator.

These references outside the Bible have led historians to a consensus—Jesus was a real person. Even Bart Ehrman, one of the most zealous critics of the Bible alive today, acknowledges Jesus lived. He wrote:

> With respect to Jesus, we have numerous, independent accounts of his life in the sources lying behind the Gospels (and the writings of Paul)—sources that originated in Jesus' native tongue Aramaic and that can be dated to within just a year or two of his life...Historical sources like that are pretty astounding for an ancient figure of any kind...the claim that Jesus was simply made up falters on every ground.[65]

Yes it does.

In light of this evidence for Jesus, you can imagine my shock when reading Richard Dawkins's book, *The God Delusion*, to see him talk about Jesus with the same qualifier he used with

65. Bart Ehrman, "Did Jesus Exist?" http://www.huffingtonpost.com/bart-d-ehrman/did-jesus-exist_b_1349544.html.

David—"if he existed."[66] If Jesus existed?—*If?* Maybe Richard should call Bart.

Another example of an incident in the Bible that has extra-biblical corroboration concerns Herod Agrippa I. He was the grandson of Herod the Great and the one who had James (the brother of John) killed and Peter imprisoned (Acts 12:1–4). In the Book of Acts (12:21) we read that Agrippa was "arrayed in royal apparel" and "sat upon his throne" to address the people in the theater at Caesarea, just inland from the Mediterranean Sea in Israel.[67] After Agrippa's speech, Luke reported that:

> The people kept crying out, "The voice of a god and not of a man!" And immediately an angel of the Lord struck him because he did not give God the glory, and he was eaten by worms and died.[68]

In his *Antiquities of the Jews*, written in approximately AD 90, long after Luke's writing, Flavius Josephus confirmed the historicity of Luke's account. He wrote:

> Now when Agrippa had reigned three years over all Judea, he came to the city Caesarea…a great multitude was got-

---

66. Richard Dawkins, *The God Delusion* (2006), 250.

67. Archaeologists have excavated this theater. See it here: http://www.bibleplaces.com/caesarea.htm.

68. Acts 12:22–23. Luke, a physician (Colossians 4:14), may have had in mind tape-worms or intestinal roundworms that can obstruct the intestines, causing severe pain, copious vomiting, and finally death.

ten together of the principal persons, and such as were of dignity...he put on a garment made wholly of silver, and of a contexture truly wonderful, and came into the theater early in the morning; at which time the silver of his garment being illuminated by the fresh reflection of the Sun's rays upon it, shone out after a surprising manner, and was so resplendent...and presently his flatterers cried out, one from one place, and another from another, (though not for his good), that he was a god...Upon this the king did neither rebuke them, nor reject their impious flattery...A severe pain also arose in his belly, and began in a most violent manner...And when he had been quite worn out by the pain in his belly for five days, he departed this life, being in the fifty-fourth year of his age, and in the seventh year of his reign.[69]

Here again, we have an extrabiblical account corroborating some of the details of a Biblical event. Josephus's account verifies that Herod Agrippa was an actual person and that he died at Caesarea shortly after the people repeatedly yelled out that he was a god.

Now, of course, extrabiblical sources don't just corroborate New Testament details; they confirm numerous Old Testament events as well. Take the Flood (Genesis 6–8) for example.

Archaeologists have unearthed a number of ancient extrabiblical writings describing a catastrophic flood. Many people

....
69. Flavius Josephus, *The Antiquities of The Jews*, Book 19, Chapter 8:2.

who scoff at the Bible's account of the Flood don't realize that the Sumerians, Assyrians, Babylonians, Greeks, Hindus, Chinese, Mexicans, Algonquins and Hawaiians all have ancient accounts of a devastating flood. Although there are some differences among the accounts, the parallels are striking. Consider this list of similarities between the Genesis Flood and the flood account known as *The Epic of Gilgamesh*, found 150 years ago in the ancient ruins of a library at Nineveh.[70] In both accounts:

- The flood was divinely planned
- The flood was connected with the defection of the human race from God or the gods
- Advance notice of the flood was given to one individual
- There was instruction to build a boat
- The boat was covered with a waterproofing pitch (tar like substance) inside and out
- A storm brought on the flood
- The boat builder's family and animals aboard the boat were preserved
- Everyone not on the boat was destroyed
- The boat came to rest atop a mountain
- Birds were sent out after the flood to determine if the world was habitable
- Sacrifices were offered after the flood

With so many points in common between *The Epic of Gil-*

----

70. See the "The Flood Tablet," relating part of *The Epic of Gilgamesh* here: http://www.britishmuseum.org/explore/highlights/highlight_objects/me/t/the_flood_tablet.aspx.

gamesh and the Biblical account, it's not difficult to conclude—as many have—that both accounts recall a common event—the Flood recorded for us in the Book of Genesis.[71]

Other historical sources outside of the Bible corroborate details surrounding:

- Long life spans prior to the Flood[72]
- The confusion of language as we have in the Biblical account of the Tower of Babel (Genesis 11:1–9)[73]
- The Exodus as confirmed by the Roman historian Tacitus[74] and Josephus[75] (who also quotes an Egyptian historian named Manetho who mentions it[76])
- The campaign into Israel by Pharaoh Shishak (1 Kings

....

71. I address critics' questions about some of the differences in the accounts and claims that Moses plagiarized other sources in my book *Archaeological Evidence for the Bible* (2012), 32–37.

72. Claims of long life spans among the ancients have been found in the records of the Egyptians, Babylonians, Greeks, Romans, Indians, and Chinese. Dr. Bryant Wood points out, "The Sumerian King List, for example, lists kings who reigned for long periods of time. Then a great Flood came. Following the Flood, Sumerian kings ruled for much shorter periods of time. This is the same pattern found in the Bible. Men had long life spans before the Flood and shorter life spans after the Flood." Source: "Is There Any Confirmation of Biblical Events From Written Sources Outside the Bible?" http://christiananswers.net/q-abr/abr-a009.html.

73. See Walter C. Kaiser, *The Old Testament Documents* (2001), 79–80; Charles Aling, "Cultural Change and the Confusion of Language in Ancient Sumer," https://www.biblearchaeology.org/post/2009/09/21/Cultural-Change-and-the-Confusion-of-Language-in-Ancient-Sumer.aspx.

74. Cornelius Tacitus wrote that most of his sources were in agreement that there was an Exodus from Egypt led by a man named "Moses." Tacitus, *Histories*, Book 5, 3–5. As to why there is not more evidence for the Exodus, see my book *Archaeological Evidence for the Bible*, 39–47.

75. Flavius Josephus, *The Antiquities of the Jews*, Book 2, Chapter 15ff.

76. Flavius Josephus, *Against Apion*, Book 1, Chapter 14–16.

14:25–26), as recorded on the walls of the Temple of
Amun in Thebes, Egypt

- Revolt of Moab against Israel (2 Kings 1:1, 3:4–27), as
recorded on the Mesha Inscription (also known as the
Moabite Stone) in the Louvre Museum
- Fall of Samaria (2 Kings 17:3–6, 24, 18:9–11) to Sargon II,
king of Assyria, as recorded on his palace walls
- Defeat of Ashdod by Sargon II (Isaiah 20:1), as recorded
on his palace walls
- Campaign of the Assyrian king Sennacherib against
Judah (2 Kings 18:13–16), as recorded on the Taylor
Prism in the British Museum
- Siege of Lachish by Sennacherib (2 Kings 18:14, 17), as
recorded on the Lachish reliefs
- Assassination of Sennacherib by his own sons (2 Kings
19:37), as recorded in the annals of his son Esarhaddon
- Fall of Nineveh as predicted by the prophets Nahum
(1:1–3:19) and Zephaniah (2:13–15), as recorded on
the Tablet of Nabopolassar in the British Museum
- Fall of Jerusalem to Nebuchadnezzar, king of Babylon
(2 Kings 24:10–14), as recorded in the Babylonian
Chronicle Tablets
- Captivity of Jehoiachin, king of Judah, in Babylon
(2 Kings 24:15–16), as recorded on the Babylonian
Ration Records
- Fall of Babylon to the Medes and Persians (Daniel
5:30–31), as recorded on the Cyrus Cylinder in the
British Museum

- Freeing of captives in Babylon by Cyrus the Great (Ezra 1:1–4; 6:3–4), as recorded on the Cyrus Cylinder[77]
- The revolt against Rome led by "Judas of Galilee"[78] the founder of the Zealots (Acts 5:37) as recorded by Josephus[79]
- The prolonged mid-day darkness on the day Jesus died (Mark 15:33), as recorded by the Roman historian Thallus (c. AD 50), a Greek author named Phlegon, Julius Africanus, and Tertullian[80]
- The "great famine" in Israel (Acts 11:28) as recorded by Josephus, Tacitus, and Suetonius[81]
- The expulsion of the Jews from Rome by the emperor Claudius (Acts 18:2) as recorded by Suetonius[82]

Friend, these are just a few examples—all written about *outside* the Bible. Critics of the Bible who brush off the Biblical accounts

---

77. Special thanks to archaeologist Dr. Bryant Wood. Many of the above points are taken from his article, "Is There Any Confirmation of Biblical Events From Written Sources Outside the Bible?" http://christiananswers.net/q-abr/abr-a009.html.

78. Not to be confused with the Judas who betrayed Jesus.

79. Flavius Josephus, *The Wars of the Jews*, Book 2, Chapter 8:118.

80. For more on this, see William Lane Craig, "Thallus on the Darkness at Noon," http://www.reasonablefaith.org/thallus-on-the-darkness-at-noon; Gary Habermas, *The Historical Jesus* (1999), 196–197; Lee Strobel, *The Case for Christ* (1998), 84–85. The darkness could not have been the result of an eclipse because an eclipse can not take place during a full moon, as was the case during the Jewish Passover season, the time of Jesus's crucifixion. Africanus points this out as well.

81. Josephus, *Antiquities*, Book 20, Chapter 5:2. Tacitus, *Annals*, Book 12:43. Suetonius, *The Twelve Caesars: Divus Claudius*, 18.

82. Suetonius, *The Twelve Caesars: Divus Claudius*, 25. For commentary on this, see Habermas, *The Historical Jesus* (1996), 190–191; Gregory Boyd and Paul Eddy, *Lord or Legend?* (2007), 124.

as mere legends or "ancient fiction"[83] only reveal how unfamiliar they are with these historical sources. If you'd like to learn more about these sources, there are several good books that discuss them.[84]

Evidence No. 5
THE BIBLE'S SCIENTIFIC ACCURACY AND FORESIGHT
Scientifically Sound

A fifth reason you can be confident in the Bible is its incredible scientific accuracy and foresight. Of course, many critics of the Bible would disagree that it's scientifically accurate. They point to Joshua 10:13 that says "the Sun stood still" or John's reference to "the four corners of the Earth" in Revelation 7:1 and they conclude the Bible teaches that the Sun revolves around a flat four-cornered Earth.

Well, they are overlooking the fact that the writers of the Bible were not writing a technical textbook on astronomy. They were describing things as they appeared to the eye (as was the case in Joshua 10) or employing normal figures of speech, as was the case with John's reference to the "four corners of the Earth."

....

83. Richard Dawkins, *The God Delusion* (2006), 97.

84. Start with Joseph Holden and Norman Geisler, *The Popular Handbook of Archaeology and the Bible* (2013) and then note their bibliography, 409–411.

And we, living in this scientifically advanced age, still do the same thing. We don't wake up early in the morning, throw open the Eastern window and say, "What a beautiful Earth revolve!" No. We say, "What a beautiful sunrise!" Technically speaking, that is unscientific terminology. Meteorologists tell us on the nightly news what time the "sunset" will be. We don't accuse them of being unscientific. They're using simple, straightforward language to describe the way things appear.

When the apostle John referred to the "four corners of the Earth" in Revelation 7:1 he was using a figure of speech to describe the extremities of the land in the four cardinal directions: North, South, East, and West. And we still use this figure of speech today. News agencies boast how they have sent their reporters out to the "four corners of the Earth" to track down their stories.[85]

So, keeping in mind that the writers of the Bible often described things in simple terms as they appeared to the eye, and that they employed figures of speech—metaphors, personification, and such—does away with many of the alleged scientific inaccuracies in the Bible.

Now, granted, Scripture is out-of-sync with some of the *philosophies* and *theories* some scientists hold to. The most obvious being atheistic naturalism and the theory of biological macro-evolution. If a scientist believes the universe, the galaxies, the Earth, and its myriad of complex life forms came

----

85. For example, see this Associated Press article: http://www.ap.org/Content/AP-In-The-News/2012/AP-veteran-reporter-Don-Rothberg-dies-at-79.

into being from "literally nothing"[86] and by nothing and then evolved to its current state via a mindless series of unguided natural causes, then yes!—the Bible, that says God created all these things, is out-of-sync with that. That goes without saying. But when it comes to known, *testable, verifiable facts*, the Bible has been found to be in perfect harmony with the way things really are, which is astonishing if you think about it. Because, as you know, the Bible was written two to four thousand years ago, long before the invention of microscopes, telescopes, satellites, and other technologies that have allowed us to investigate our Earth and the universe.

The fact that the Bible was written so long ago, touches on a myriad of topics, and yet does not contain any scientific errors, might be considered evidence for divine inspiration all on its own. Why? Without exception, every ancient religious writing has certain unscientific views of astronomy, medicine, hygiene, and so on. For example, the Hindu Vedas teach that the Earth is flat and triangular.[87] They also teach that the Earth rests on the backs of elephants that stand on the back of a turtle[88] that's supported by a serpent floating in a boundless ocean.[89] The Quran speaks of a man traveling until he finds the place the Sun descends down into the Earth. It says he traveled "till

86. Richard Dawkins, "Something from Nothing and the Magic of Reality" Part 2. http://www.youtube.com/watch?v=ygXDWOp2vgs.

87. Donald Lach and Edwin Van Kley, *Asia in the Making of Europe, Vol. 3: A Century of Advance* (1993), 782.

88. Some sources say it's a turtle, others a tortoise.

89. Patrick Moore, *The Great Astronomical Revolution: 1534-1687 and the Space Age Epilogue* (1994), 24.

when he reached the setting-place of the Sun, he found it setting in a muddy spring."[90] This is an error of astronomical proportions. The Sun—as we now know—is thousands of times bigger than the Earth and 93 million miles away from the planet. But Muhammad could get away with a statement like that in certain parts of the world in the seventh century.

Other scientific errors in the Quran include:

- A hard sky that can fall on the inhabitants of the Earth (22:65, 34:9)
- Stars that fly away when Abraham glances at them (37:88–90)
- A moon that is further away than the stars (67:3, 5 and 71:15–16)

And there are more.[91]

The Bible steers free of these kinds of errors. But not only that, it makes known amazing facts about our world and the universe thousands of years before scientists discovered they were actually true. Allow me to share with you five examples.

....

90. Quran 18:86. Muslims who seek to reinterpret what this verse means, are often stunned to learn that Muhammad, speaking outside of the Quran (in the Hadith) confirms that he meant exactly what this verse says. He asks a man, Abu Dharr, "Do you know where this [Sun] sets? It sets in a spring of murky water, [then] it goes and prostrates before its Lord, the Exalted in Might and the Ever-Majestic, under the Throne." For more on this see: http://www.answering-islam.org/authors/shamoun/mhmd_on_sunset.html.

91. To learn about additional errors in the Quran, see Jay Smith, "Errors Which Contradict Secular and Scientific Data," http://www.debate.org.uk/debate-topics/historical/does-the-bible/#13.

A. The Start of the Universe

Aristotle (384–322 BC) and many of the Greeks regarded the universe as eternal and uncreated. Aristotle condemned the idea that the universe came into being at some point in time as unthinkable.[92] And up until the last century, the prevailing scientific theory was that Aristotle was right! The universe was eternal; it had always existed. Well, that view has fallen on hard times. In fact, the scientific evidence against an eternal universe has demolished this view. Astronomers are pointing to things like the background radiation echo, the second law of thermodynamics, the motion of the galaxies, and other evidences, all of which have led them to conclude the universe had a beginning. Discussing all these evidences is outside the scope of this little book, but the consensus amongst the majority of astronomers today is that the universe *began* to exist—it's not eternal.

That's interesting because this is in perfect harmony with what the Bible says. Where? The very first verse! Genesis 1:1 says, "In the *beginning* God created the heavens and the earth." The Bible makes it clear here and elsewhere[93] that the universe actually had a beginning, exactly like the scientific community has finally discovered—more than 3000 years after Moses penned those words. They would have known this a lot sooner had they read the Bible.

Arno Penzias, who was awarded a Nobel Prize for discovering evidence that the universe had a beginning, agrees that

92. Rodney Stark, *The Triumph of Christianity* (2011), 286. See Aristotle, *Physics* (Book 8), http://classics.mit.edu/Aristotle/physics.8.viii.html.

93. For example, 2 Peter 3:4 mentions "the *beginning* of creation."

the scientific data lines right up with the Bible. He said, "The best data we have are exactly what I would have predicted, had I nothing to go on but the five books of Moses, the Psalms and the Bible as a whole."[94]

B. The Sun

Writing about the Sun in Psalm 19:6, David said, "Its rising is from one end of the heavens, and its *circuit* to the other end of them." For years critics scoffed at this verse thinking it taught geocentricity—that the Sun revolves around the Earth. They said, "The Sun doesn't go anywhere. It's stationary and the Earth moves around the Sun!" However, it has been discovered in more recent times that the Sun *does* move. It's traveling about 52,000 miles per hour on a circuit through the heavens as it makes its way around the center of the Milky Way Galaxy[95]—all in perfect harmony with what the Bible says here in Psalm 19:6.

C. The Shape of the Earth

Long before the Greeks figured out the world was round, the ancient Egyptians, Babylonians, and Chinese believed the world was flat.[96] Remarkably, the Bible went against the prevailing views of the day and indicated the Earth was a sphere. In the Book of Job, thought to be written about 2000 BC, Job tells

94. Arno Penzias in interview with Malcolm Browne, "Clues To The Universe's Origin Expected," *New York Times*, March 12, 1978, 1.

95. Andrew Fazekas, "Sun is Moving Slower Than Thought," http://news.nationalgeographic.com/news/2012/05/120510-sun-slower-bow-shock-heliosphere-nasa-ibex-space-science.

96. Abby Cessna, "Flat Earth Theory," http://www.universetoday.com/48753/flat-earth-theory.

us that God "has inscribed a *circle* on the surface of the waters at the boundary of light and darkness" (26:10). Fascinating! Job says God has drawn "a circle" on "the surface" of the waters (the oceans) at the "boundary of light and darkness." This boundary between light and darkness is where evening and morning occur. Notice the boundary is not a square or a triangle. It's a circle. Why? Because the Earth is round. Another verse that speaks of the circular shape of the Earth is found in Isaiah 40:22, written about 700 BC: "It is He [God] who sits above the *circle* of the Earth."

SKEPTIC: "Well, then why was the Catholic Church still trying to convince people the world was flat at the time of Columbus in 1492?"

It wasn't. The Catholic Church never espoused a flat Earth at the time of Christopher Columbus or any time prior to that. This is a legend fabricated by Washington Irving in 1828 in his largely fictional biography of Christopher Columbus.[97] No educated Europeans at the time of Columbus believed in a flat Earth—and for good reason. As Dr. Jeffrey Russell, Professor of History, Emeritus, at the University of California, in Santa Barbara, points out:

A round earth appears at least as early as the sixth century BC with Pythagoras, who was followed by Aristotle, Euclid,

----

97. Rodney Stark, *The Triumph of Christianity* (2011), 274; Jeffrey Burton Russell, *Exposing Myths About Christianity* (2012), 143; Valerie Strauss, "Busting a Myth About Columbus and a Flat Earth," at washingtonpost.com, see tinyurl.com/k7vc6yr. Also see J. B. Russell's in-depth book on this topic: *Inventing the Flat Earth: Columbus and the Historians.*

and Aristarchus, among others in observing that the earth was a sphere. Although there were a few dissenters—Leukippos and Demokritos for example—by the time of Eratosthenes (3 c. BC), followed by Crates (2 c. BC), Strabo (3 c. BC), and Ptolemy (first c. AD), the sphericity of the earth was accepted by all educated Greeks and Romans.[98]

And it wasn't just secular Greeks and Romans who believed this. Dr. Russell points out that tens of thousands of Christian theologians, poets, artists, and scientists believed the Earth was a sphere throughout the early, medieval, and modern church.[99] From the time of the early church up until the time of Columbus, a span of about 1200 years, only two known Christian writers (who had no followers) asserted the Earth was flat and more than a hundred attested it was round.[100]

D. The Suspension of the Earth

As I mentioned earlier, Hindus once believed the Earth rested on the backs of elephants who stood on the back of a turtle.[101] Some of the ancient Greeks believed the mythical god Atlas carried the Earth on his shoulders (a burden given to him

....

98. Jeffrey Burton Russell, "The Myth of the Flat Earth," http://www.veritas-ucsb.org/library/russell/FlatEarth.html.

99. Ibid.

100. Jeffrey Burton Russell, *Exposing Myths About Christianity* (2012), 142–143.

101. Michael Allaby, National Geographic's *Visual Encyclopedia of Earth* (2008), 246; Stephen Law, *Philosophy* (2007), 213.

as punishment by Zeus).[102] *Something* has to support the Earth they reasoned. What did the Bible say? In one of the oldest books in the Bible, Job said, "He [God] stretches out the north over *empty* space and hangs the earth on *nothing*" (Job 26:7). Nothing! In other words, the Earth hangs completely unattached in space. This is astounding. Scientists were still trying to figure this out thousands of years later.[103]

E. The Stars

Before the invention of the telescope, people believed the stars could all be numbered. People were so confident of this, they drew up star charts with all the known stars named and numbered. The Greek astronomer and mathematician Hipparchus (190–120 BC) claimed there were 1026 stars.[104] The astronomer and mathematician Ptolemy (c. AD 85–165) stated there were 1056 stars.[105] The German astronomer Johannes Kepler (1571–1630) counted 1005.[106] When Galileo (a devout Christian) pointed his telescope to the heavens in 1608, he discovered these previous counts were way off and the Bible was actually right. What did the Scriptures have to say regarding the matter?

In Jeremiah 33:22, God declared, "The host of heaven [a ref-

....

102. Mark Cartwright, "Atlas," *Ancient History Encyclopedia*, http://www.ancient.eu-.com/Atlas. Also Sir Thomas Heath, *Greek Astronomy* (1932, reprint 1991), 170.

103. See "Kepler's Laws of Planetary Motion" or "Celestial Mechanics" in *The Encyclopedia Britannica* (2013), http://www.britannica.com.

104. François Arago, *Popular Astronomy*, Vol. 1 (1855), 213.

105. Ben Hobrink, *Modern Science in the Bible* (2011), 124.

106. Ibid. Some say the number was 1006.

erence to the stars] cannot be numbered, nor the sand of the sea measured." God says the stars cannot be numbered. In fact, trying to do so would be about as futile as trying to count the grains of sand floating around in the sea, obviously an impossible task. Jeremiah wrote that more than 2000 years before Galileo made his discovery.

Today, with the help of powerful telescopes, astronomers tell us the universe contains somewhere between 100 billion and a trillion galaxies containing anywhere between 100 billion and 10 trillion stars each.[107] That's a lot of stars!

A new study, published in the journal *Nature*, suggests there are a mind-blowing 300 sextillion stars in the universe.[108] When the estimate was at a measly 70 sextillion stars in 2003, scientists said there were "10 times as many stars as grains of sand on all the world's beaches and deserts."[109] I don't know what kind of beach and desert analogies they'll suggest next, but surely "the host of heaven cannot be numbered" (Jeremiah 33:22).

Now, these kinds of statements in the Bible about the stars, Earth, Sun, and universe raise a question—how in the world did the authors of the Bible living so long ago know these kinds of things? Were they taking wild guesses? No. Their perfect accuracy rules that out, especially when you consider the fact that

....

107. Seth Borenstein, "Starry Starry Starry Night: Star Count May Triple," Wednesday, December 1, 2010, http://www.washingtontimes.com/news/2010/dec/1/starry-starry-starry-night-star-count-may-triple.

108. Ibid. That's a 3 followed by 23 zeros. To arrive at that number, just take 3 trillion and multiply it by 100 billion.

109. "Star Survey Reaches 70 Sextillion," July 23, 2003, http://www.cnn.com/2003/TECH/space/07/22/stars.survey.

there are dozens of statements like these in the Bible concerning these matters.[110]

The apostle Peter told us how they knew these things when he wrote, "Men moved by the Holy Spirit spoke from God" (2 Peter 1:21).[111] God, who knows all there is to know about the universe He created, superintended (came along side) the writing of the Bible to make sure what the authors penned accurately reflected the way things really are.

SKEPTIC: "Well, if the Bible is so accurate regarding these matters, why aren't more scientists Christians? It seems to me that Christianity and science are incompatible."

Good question. Dr. Jeffrey Russell, who I quoted a few pages ago, points out:

The answer to "Why aren't more scientists Christians?" might be the same as the one to "Why aren't more real estate agents Christians?" They go with the current, and the current flows where the going is easiest....If it were true that Christianity and science were incompatible, there would be no Christians who were respected scientists. In fact, about forty percent of professional natural scientists are practicing Christians, and many others are theists of other kinds.

---

110. John Ankerberg and Dillon Burroughs have a summary list of them in their book *Taking a Stand for the Bible* (2009), 103–109; Also see Ben Hobrink, *Modern Science in the Bible.*

111. *The King James Version* reads, "Holy men of God spoke as they were moved by the Holy Spirit." *The English Standard Version* says, "Men spoke from God as they were carried along by the Holy Spirit."

Fewer than thirty percent are atheists.[112]

In 2011, Rodney Stark, one of the leading authorities on the sociology of religion, noted that "The majority of American scientists still report themselves to be religious."[113] Because that is the case, a better question might be, "If it's so clear God doesn't exist, and belief in God is "delusional"—to quote Richard Dawkins[114]—why do so many scientists believe in God?"

The truth of the matter is that Christianity is *not* incompatible with science. As Dr. Russell notes, "Christianity has not been the enemy of science; in fact, sustained scientific development originated in Christian Europe"[115] primarily with Bible believing Christians like Johannes Kepler, Galileo Galilei, Francis Bacon, Blaise Pascal, Isaac Newton, and Michael Faraday—some of the greatest scientists ever. And there are brilliant scientists today who find the teachings of the Bible perfectly compatible with their desire to investigate the world scientifically.[116] One of them, John Lennox, a professor and scientist at Oxford University, says:

Many people have the wrong impression that Christianity is

....

112. Jeffrey Burton Russell, *Exposing Myths About Christianity* (2012), 142.

113. Rodney Stark, *The Triumph of Christianity* (2011), 294.

114. Richard Dawkins, *The God Delusion* (2006), 15.

115. Russell, *Exposing*, 149. He explains *why* it developed in Christian Europe and not elsewhere on pages 149–153. Also see Stark, *Triumph* (2011), 271–295.

116. Some of the more well-known ones are Michael Behe, Walter Bradley, Francis Collins, William Dembski, Jason Lisle, Stephen Meyer, Hugh Ross, Henry Schaefer.

anti-intellectual, and it is only for people with a weak mind. And I think that is completely wrong. I am a scientist; I believe in God. I want to show that those two things can go together. But above all, I want to show that the Bible can be taken seriously without committing intellectual suicide.[117]

SKEPTIC: "But if the Bible is to be taken seriously regarding these kinds of things, how do you justify the Catholic Church imprisoning and torturing Galileo for teaching that the Earth revolves around the Sun? That seems to me to be a prime example of people who take the Bible seriously standing in the way of scientific progress!"

Well, first off, I don't try to justify what the Catholic Church did to Galileo (1564–1642). And neither does any Christian I know. Even the Catholic Church has apologized for their treatment of Galileo.[118] But it would be good to make sure we have our facts straight about what actually happened to Galileo.

Despite Carl Sagan's statement about him being "in a Catholic dungeon" where he was "threatened...with torture"[119] or the Indigo Girls singing, "Galileo's head was on the block,"[120]

117. John Lennox, "Science and Ethics: Exclusive interview with John Lennox," http://www.christiantelegraph.com/issue18880.html.

118. "The Galileo Affair," http://www.vaticanobservatory.org/index.php/en/history-of-astronomy/197-the-galileo-affair.

119. Carl Sagan, *Cosmos* (1980), Kindle edition, 1224.

120. "Galileo" by the Indigo Girls, http://www.indigogirls.com/discographyandlyrics/lyrics/ritesofpassage.html.

Galileo "was never in a dungeon or tortured."[121] This is widely acknowledged today in biographies on Galileo, history books, the *Encyclopedia Britannica*, etc. Galileo was sentenced to a rather comfortable house arrest in his villa near Florence, Italy.[122] He was allowed to continue working and writing, and the Catholic Church even continued giving him his pension[123] until he died "peacefully in his bed"[124] nine years later at the age of 77 in 1642. Don't misunderstand me—I disagree with how Galileo was treated. No one wants to have their ideas rejected and be confined to their home. So, I'm not seeking to justify what happened, only to lay to rest the legends of Galileo being tortured in a dungeon.

But something else needs to be pointed out. The Catholic Church's opposition to Galileo is only part of the story. Do you know who else rejected Galileo and his discoveries? The brightest intellectuals, secular philosophers, and academic professors of his day![125] I never see this mentioned on atheists' websites. And I think I know why. It takes all the wind out of their "Christians were standing in the way of scientific progress" propaganda.

....

121. "Galileo," http://www.britannica.com/EBchecked/topic/224058/Galileo/8441/Galileos-Copernicanism. For more on this, see: Rodney Stark, *The Triumph of Christianity* (2011), 289; Jeffrey Burton Russell, *Exposing Myths About Christianity* (2012), 133.

122. Stark, *Triumph* (2011), 289; Russell, *Exposing* (2012), 137.

123. Jay Richards in Lee Strobel, *The Case for a Creator* (2004), 163.

124. Alfred North Whitehead, *Science and the Modern World* (1997), 2.

125. John Lennox, *God's Undertaker: Has Science Buried God?* (2009), 24; Jeffrey Burton Russell, *Exposing Myths About Christianity* (2012), 133–137.

Galileo's scientific arguments (which built upon and advanced Nicolaus Copernicus's heliocentric Sun-centered hypothesis published in 1543) threatened the all-pervading view held by the academies. The academies held to the geocentric understanding developed by Aristotle (384–322 BC) that said the Earth was at the physical center of the universe[126] and Ptolemy's (AD c. 100–c. 170) view that the Earth was stationary and the Sun revolved around it. This Aristotelian-Ptolemaic geocentric view was entrenched everywhere and it had been for 1400 years. So, it wasn't just the Church that opposed Galileo's discoveries. The brightest thinkers of the day disagreed with him, including the "secular philosophers who were enraged at his criticism of Aristotle."[127] Even Tyco Brahe (1546–1601), the greatest astronomer of the period disagreed with Galileo.[128] This widespread opposition is a hugely important part of the story that is conveniently left out whenever atheists tell the story.

And here's another fact atheists rarely mention on their websites or in their books. Galileo, often referred to as the "father of modern astronomy," the "father of modern physics," and the "father of science"[129] was—as I mentioned briefly a couple pages ago—a Christian! Not a nominal Christian; he was a firm believer in God and the Bible and remained so all of his

....

126. Lennox, *God's Undertaker*, 24.

127. Ibid.

128. Dinesh D'Souza, *What's So Great About Christianity?* (2007), 106.

129. "Astronomer Galileo dies in Italy," http://www.history.com/this-day-in-history/astronomer-galileo-dies-in-italy.

life, even after his ideas were rejected by the Catholic Church.[130] In a letter explaining his views on the mixture of science and religion, Galileo wrote: "Holy Scripture could never lie or err... its decrees are of absolute and inviolable truth."[131] And Nicolaus Copernicus (1473–1543)—the astronomer who proposed the heliocentric[132] (Sun-centered) system before Galileo—was a Christian as well, one who believed "the universe [had been] wrought for us by a supremely good and orderly Creator!"[133]

Now, obviously a lot more could be said about the history of science and evidence that agrees with the Bible. In the interest of keeping things concise here, I'll refer you to the following outstanding books:

- *God's Undertaker: Has Science Buried God?* by John Lennox
- *The Case for a Creator: A Journalist Investigates Scientific Evidence that Points Toward God* by Lee Strobel
- *The Design Revolution: Answering the Toughest Questions About Intelligent Design* by William Dembski

I've purposely arranged the first five chapters in the order I have so that if you can remember the acronym **F.A.C.E.S.**, you'll have an easier time remembering these evidences.

....

130. Lennox, *God's Undertaker*, 24–26.

131. Quoted in Stillman Drake, *Galileo at Work: His Scientific Biography* (1978), 224.

132. Heliocentric (or "Sun-centered") is derived from the Greek *helios*, meaning "Sun."

133. Quoted in Charles Hummel, *The Galileo Connection* (1986), 39.

F.A.C.E.S.

F = Fulfilled Prophecy
A = Archaeological Evidence
C = Consistency (Internal Harmony)
E = Extrabiblical Writings
S = Scientific Accuracy and Foresight

I have found this acronym helpful, in that it gives me a bit of a framework to work from in my mind as I talk to a person for a minute or two about each of these different lines of evidence. I hope you'll find it helpful as well.

Evidence No. 6
THE MANUSCRIPT EVIDENCE
Scrolls & Scribes

Critics of the Bible commonly say its words have been translated and copied so many times down through the centuries we can't trust what it says today—even if the Bible was once trustworthy. Well, as popular as this belief may be, it's a mistaken one. Allow me to show you why scholars know that to be the case. I'll start with a simple illustration.

Let's say for Christmas I send you a Christmas card and inside I include for you a hand written 3" by 5" card with my favorite chocolate chip cookie recipe. We'll call it "Charlie's Chocolate Chip Cookie Concoction." Now, you have the original penned by the author, right? Right.

A short time later, you make the cookies for family and friends gathered at your home for a Christmas party and they love them. So, you copy the recipe by hand on to 3" by 5" cards for all twenty of your guests. They love the cookies so much, soon after they do the same thing. They hand write a bunch of copies of the recipe and send them to all their friends. This repeats itself over and over for decades.

Five hundred years from now "Charlie's Chocolate Chip Cookie Concoction" has spread to countries all over the world. The year is 2514 when someone discovers the recipe for the first time. He's flabbergasted with how good the cookies taste but begins to wonder if his copy of the recipe is an accurate reflection of what the original said hundreds of years before. So, what does he do? He grabs his Indiana Jones hat (yes, the movie is still loved) and begins searching the world high and low for other copies of the recipe. He goes to libraries, museums, and restaurants gathering up old copies of the recipe. He spends hundreds of hours looking through Internet databases. In the end, he's discovered and acquired hundreds of handwritten copies of the recipe in different languages from all over the world.

With expensive dating equipment he finds out that many of the copies are hundreds of years old, some much newer. A few are slightly different than others. Most say "stir." A few say "mix." Most say, "Use one teaspoon of vanilla." A couple say, "Use one tablespoon of vanilla." Some reverse the order of a word or two. Many have a word or two misspelled. Most say bake at 300 degrees, but a few say 30 degrees. Some are torn. Some of the oldest copies are pretty beat up, but a lot of them are in very good condition.

Now that the collector's search has ended, he's determined to know if his first copy of the recipe accurately reflects what the original said. He's got hundreds of copies laid out on tables before him. Question for you: What do you think the chances are he could do that? Pretty good, right?

What if he was to have the help of hundreds of experts (chefs, historians, language specialists, etc.)? Well, of course the chances the wording of the original could be known would increase even more. It would be easy for these experts to spot obvious slips of the pen that exist in some of the copies. The experts have hundreds of copies to compare and cross-check with one another. And of course, who bakes cookies at 30 degrees? This would easily be recognized as an unintentional copyist error.

Now, why the story about a cookie recipe? Well, it helps illustrate what scholars called textual critics have been able to do with the Bible. Textual critics are people who seek to reconstruct the reading of ancient documents that no longer exist using existing manuscript copies.

Over the centuries, textual critics and Bible scholars have gathered together surviving manuscript copies of the Bible and spent years examining them, comparing them with one another, seeking to increase our certainty of what the original documents said. And these scholars don't just have a few hundred manuscripts at their disposal, they have thousands and thousands!

Today there survives more than 25,000 partial and complete handwritten manuscript copies of the New Testament, many dating back to within the first century or two following Jesus's life.[134] We also possess thousands of manuscript copies of Old Testament books—many of them predating the time of Christ. Did you know that? There are handwritten copies of the Old Testament, copied by scribes prior to Jesus's birth, that still survive to this day!

In 1947 a shepherd boy tending his father's flock in Qumran, north and to the west of the Dead Sea in Israel, made an amazing discovery while looking for a lost goat. There in Qumran, in a hillside cave that had laid untouched for nearly two thousand years, this twelve-year-old Muslim boy discovered a collection of large clay jars containing carefully wrapped leather manuscripts. What this boy stumbled upon was an ancient collection of handwritten copies of the Old Testament that dated as far back as the third century before Christ.[135] This was an incredible discovery!

Archaeologists spent years searching the surrounding caves. By the time they were done, copies of every book of the Old Testament had been discovered (with the exception of

....

134. Daniel Wallace notes that altogether, there are currently more than 2.6 million pages of New Testament manuscripts. The average Greek NT manuscript is more than 450 pages long! Wallace, *Revisiting the Corruption of the New Testament*, 28.

135. Walter Kaiser, *The Old Testament Documents* (2001), 41.

the Book of Esther). In some cases there were multiple copies of the same book. For example, there were nineteen copies of the Book of Isaiah, twenty-five copies of Deuteronomy and thirty copies of the Psalms.[136]

SKEPTIC: "Hold on Charlie. How do they know the Dead Sea Scrolls were really that old?"

Good question. The great archaeologist Dr. William F. Albright and other scholars determined the age of the scrolls by carefully examining the weave and pattern of the manuscript cloths, the form of the Hebrew characters, the spelling of the words, and the pottery that housed the manuscripts. The clay jars were Late Hellenistic (c. 150–63 BC) and Early Roman (c. 63 BC to AD 100). They also examined the coins found alongside the manuscripts. The inscriptions on the coins showed that they were minted between 135 BC and AD 68.[137] And, more recently, accelerator mass spectrometry testing was done on the scrolls at the University of Arizona, again confirming their antiquity.[138]

The Dead Sea Scrolls and hundreds of other manuscripts dating back to the time of the early church, have allowed Biblical scholars, translators, and textual critics to recover with a very high degree of certainty the text of the Bible that Jesus quoted and the early Christians used 2000 years ago.

....

136. Mark Water, *Encyclopedia of Bible Facts* (2004), 138.

137. Edwin Yamauchi, *The Stones and the Scriptures: An Introduction to Biblical Archaeology* (1981), 129.

138. See the article "Radiocarbon Dating of Fourteen Dead Sea Scrolls" online here: https://journals.uair.arizona.edu/index.php/radiocarbon/article/viewFile/1537/1541. For more on the dating of the Dead Sea Scrolls, see Norman Geisler and William Nix, *From God to Us: How We Got Our Bible* (2012), 201–202.

If you'd like to, you can see these manuscripts with your own eyes at the British Museum, Cambridge University Library, Oxford University, the Israel Museum in Jerusalem, and even online at the Center for the Study of New Testament Manuscripts website.[139] And if you know a little Greek or Hebrew, you can look at these manuscripts and see what they said all the way back in the first, second, and third centuries and compare them with what the Bible says today. And you'll discover the Bible says the same thing today it did long ago. Are there some tiny spelling variations, slips of the pen, and grammatical mistakes in some of the manuscripts? Yes. Are there accidental omissions and additions in some of them? Yes. Are there different arrangements of the words in some? Yes. But none of these variants have kept scholars from being able to reconstruct what the original documents said.[140]

Remember, even when a manuscript copy has errors in it, there are thousands of other manuscripts to cross-check it with. And none of these spelling errors, word additions, or omissions ever affect "an article of faith or a precept of duty which is not abundantly sustained by other and undoubted passages, or by the whole tenor of Scripture teaching."[141] Even the vocal critic of the Bible, Bart Ehrman, author of the *New York Times* bestseller *Misquoting Jesus*, acknowledges this. Tucked away in the back of

....

139. www.csntm.org.

140. And remember, these variants do nothing to harm the doctrine of inerrancy, for as Norman Geisler writes, inerrancy "does not mean that every copy and translation of the Bible is perfect. God breathed out the originals, not the copies, so inerrancy applies to the original text, not to every copy." *Baker Encyclopedia of Apologetics* (1999), 93.

141. Lewis Sperry Chafer, *Systematic Theology,* Vol. 1 (1976), 88.

the paperback edition of his book (when and where few readers would notice!), Ehrman acknowledges, "Essential Christian beliefs are *not affected* by textual variants in the manuscript tradition of the New Testament."[142] See that? Not affected he says. Had he stated that up front in the introduction of his book when it was first released, the book would have never made the bestseller list. We probably wouldn't even know who Ehrman was. But alas, it appears the temptation to be sensational was too much.

Quotations By the Church Fathers

Now, it's also important to point out that even if we did not have any surviving manuscript copies of the Bible, there is another way of verifying we have accurate copies of the Bible, and that is by examining the writings of the early church fathers. I'm referring to the leaders in the church of the first three centuries following the original disciples. Men like Ignatius, Papias, Justin Martyr, Irenaeus, Polycarp, and others preserved the Bible for us in their writings, commentaries, and sermons. How? By including numerous quotations of the Bible in what they wrote. In fact, they quoted the New Testament alone more than 86,000 times.[143] If you count the quotations of the church fathers up through the thirteenth century, there are more than a *million*

142. Bart Ehrman, *Misquoting Jesus* (Paperback edition, appendix), 252. Italics added.

143. This number was calculated by Oxford professor John William Burgon. See Josh McDowell, "Hasn't the New Testament Changed?" http://www.josh.org/resources/study-research/answers-to-skeptics-questions/hasnt-the-new-testament-changed. For more on Burgon, see: http://www.ccel.org/ccel/burgon.

quotations.[144] And here's something a lot of people don't realize. Many of the church fathers' writings survive to this day! You can go to Amazon.com and buy an encyclopedic size set of the writings of the church fathers (38 volumes) and see with your own eyes their numerous quotations of both the Old and New Testaments.

In fact, there are enough quotations from the early church fathers that even if we did not have a single surviving manuscript copy of the Bible, we could still reconstruct the New Testament today just from their writings. Dr. Norman Geisler, author of 80 plus books on the Bible and related topics, says, "It is an amazing fact that the New Testament could be reconstructed simply from quotations made within two hundred years of its composition."[145]

The internationally renowned textual critic and Bible scholar at Princeton, Dr. Bruce Metzger agreed, "Indeed, so extensive are these citations that if all other sources for our knowledge of the text of the New Testament were destroyed, they would be sufficient alone for the reconstruction of practically the entire New Testament."[146]

Dr. Daniel Wallace, Executive Director of the Center for the Study of New Testament Manuscripts, adds: "The whole New Testament is duplicated more than once in these [pre-thirteenth

....

144. Daniel Wallace, *Revisiting the Corruption of the New Testament* (2011), 28.

145. Norman Geisler and William Nix, *From God to Us: How We Got Our Bible* (2012), 218.

146. Bruce Metzger and Bart Ehrman, *The Text of the New Testament* (2005), 126.

century] church fathers' writings."[147]

So, the church fathers' quotations serve as an additional verification that we have accurate copies of the Bible in our possession today.

Friend, the fact that the Scriptures are still intact after more than two thousand years of transmission should not come as a surprise. Isaiah 40:8 says, "The grass withers, the flower fades, but the word of our God stands *forever*." Jesus declared in Matthew 24:35, "Heaven and earth will pass away, but My words will not pass away." Heaven and Earth will pass away before such a thing would happen to God's Word.

SKEPTIC: "This is all food for thought, but if God exists and is so eager for us to know the Bible, why didn't He just miraculously preserve the *original* documents the authors penned? Then we could know for certain that the Biblical text came down to us in a trustworthy manner!"

That's a fair question. The original documents (known as *autographs*) were written on leather scrolls, papyrus, and other materials that wouldn't last indefinitely. And so, yes, to our knowledge, none of the originals actually survive. They likely wore out through much use and turned to dust before the end of the third century.[148] But why didn't God miraculously preserve the originals?

....

147. Daniel Wallace, "The Value and Problems of Church Fathers," http://www.youtube. com/watch?v=3OZKCHVi79A. Statement is made at 1:09.

148. Daniel Wallace has an excellent article on how long the autographs likely survived and the early church fathers' references to them. See "Did the Original New Testament Manuscripts Still Exist in the Second Century?" https://bible.org/article/did-original-new-testament-manuscripts-still-exist-second-century.

Well, I don't know why God does or doesn't do certain things. He certainly could have preserved the originals. But I think God may have allowed the originals to disappear so that we could actually be *more* certain we have trustworthy copies of the Bible.

Let's imagine Paul's original letter to the Romans was allowed to survive and was in someone's possession today. Because of its importance and value, it has been locked up in a climate-controlled underground vault at some European seminary where's it gone unseen by the public since the time of the Council of Nicea (AD 325).

The person or persons who had oversight of an original like this could prevent others from seeing it, hinder people from copying it, and even change it or manipulate what it says. And who would know of the changes? Perhaps no one except those doing the changing. And then the people who had the original could one day unlock the vault, call in the Discovery Channel—they're always game for a story that might overturn Christianity—then spring the "original" upon the world and reveal that Paul advocated something completely contrary to what the original actually said. That wouldn't be good.

But, if Paul's original letter to the Romans is quickly copied numerous times all the way back in the first century and these copies are then spread all over the ancient world, and then Paul's original writing crumbles into dust, there's no way a person could alter Paul's original intent. Someone might *try* to sneak a bit of heresy into a manuscript *copy*, but the hundreds of other copies in circulation would quickly allow the churches to cross-check and compare the questionable copy with other more reliable copies. And the variants (whether they were just small slips of the pen, grammatical errors, or something more serious like word additions or omissions) would be exposed for what they were—not part of the original.

There's another reason God may have allowed the autographs to wear out and disappear. Dr. Michael Kruger, author of the book *Gospel Fragments*, summarized the problem when he wrote, "One can imagine how easily (and quickly) such documents would become objects of veneration, if not worship. They might have become the equivalent of Gideon's ephod (Judges 8:27)—a good gift the people begin to treat as an idol."[149]

Whatever reasons God has for allowing the autographs to disappear, the bottom line is this—we can be confident we have accurate copies of the Bible without them.

SKEPTIC: "Well, if we have accurate copies of the Bible today, they would only be accurate copies of the one the Roman Emperor Constantine (c. 275–337) tampered with! When he ascended to power, he had the content of the Bible changed to make sure it supported his political agenda."

Unfortunately, many people were led to think this after reading the hugely popular but error-riddled novel *The Da Vinci Code* by Dan Brown.[150] But friend, this idea that Constantine altered the text of the Bible is completely false. There's not a par-

....

149. Michael Kruger, "The Difference Between Original Autographs and Original Texts," http://thegospelcoalition.org/blogs/tgc/2013/05/15/the-difference-between -original-autographs-and-original-texts.

150. I address many of the outrageous, unfounded, provably false claims in the book at AlwaysBeReady.com. Click on "Da Vinci Code" in the main menu.

ticle of tangible data to support it. Ed Strauss, author of *Why Should I Believe the Bible?* points out:

There's absolutely no evidence that the Roman Empire changed the Scriptures. In fact, when they [critics of the Bible who raise this objection] are asked which parts of the text the Romans changed, most critics are at a loss for words. A logical assumption is that the Romans would have added passages like Romans 13:1–7, which commands Christians to be subject to the government, to not resist those in authority, to pay taxes, and to consider the authorities "God's ministers." Presumably, they would also have added 1 Peter 2:13–17 (or beefed it up if it existed), which admonishes Christians to submit to every law of man, and to "honor the king [Caesar]." The problem with this theory, however, is that the Bible as we have it today can be checked against earlier copies of the scriptures. Constantine became a Christian in AD 312 and in AD 331 ordered Eusebius to provide fifty Bibles for churches. However, copies of the scriptures exist from before these dates. The Beatty Papyrus P46 contains Romans 13, which is identical to the text we have today. Scholars date it to AD 175–225—at least eighty years before Constantine became a Christian. As for Peter's commands, the Bodmer Papyrus P72 contains the entire book of 1 Peter—including the passage 2:13–17. This document dates to AD 200, some 112 years before Constantine's conversion. The full collections of the Beatty and the Bodmer papyri contain the majority of the New Testament, and no changes that can be construed as "Roman" are evident between these and post-Constantine copies. The conclusion: The Romans didn't entertain such motives and didn't take such actions.[151]

It's also worth noting if Constantine or the Roman government had ever tampered with the Bible, the church fathers alive at the time and in the decades to follow would certainly have mentioned it in their writings. And they don't. Not a word. Because it never happened!

SKEPTIC: "Maybe Constantine didn't tamper with the text of the Bible directly, but he's the one who determined what books belonged in the Bible. And he purposely left out books that contradicted his view of what Christianity should look like."

This is absolutely not true. Constantine had nothing to do with which books were included in the Bible. The Old Testament was done, compiled, and in wide circulation amongst the Jews long before Jesus was even born, and certainly long before the time of Constantine (c. 275–337). As for the New Testament, its formation began by the end of the first century. By the end of the second century, the complete canon of Scripture *exactly as we have it today* was popularly recognized and already being quoted by the church fathers nearly a hundred years before Constantine was even born.

For more on the manuscript evidence and how believers

....

151. Ed Strauss, *Why Should I Believe the Bible?* (2013), 162–163.

recognized which books God determined should be included in the Bible, I recommend the following books:

- *From God to Us: How We Got the Bible* (2012 ed.) by Norman Geisler and William Nix
- *Who Chose the Gospels?* by C. E. Hill
- *The Canon of Scripture* by F. F. Bruce
- *The New Testament Documents: Are They Reliable?* by F. F. Bruce
- *The Old Testament Documents: Are They Reliable and Relevant?* by Walter C. Kaiser
- *Revisiting the Corruption of the New Testament* by Daniel Wallace (editor)
- *Misquoting Truth: A Guide to the Fallacies of Bart Ehrman's* Misquoting Jesus by Timothy Paul Jones

Evidence No. 7
THE BIBLE'S FORTHRIGHTNESS ABOUT ITS AUTHORS' AND CHARACTERS' FAILURES
Sexual Sin, Lying, Murder

When you look at various websites today and click on the "About Us" button, you typically encounter a carefully-crafted, glowing overview of what that company, political organization, or religious group is about. If they have an "Our History" button or "Our Founder" button, again you nearly always get a favorable overview of the founder. You never read that the founder is an adulterer or has a criminal record—for obvious reasons. Of course, they are not necessarily seeking to be deceitful by withholding that kind of information, they just understand that kind of information is not necessary for customers to know; it could hurt their business, scare off investors, etc.

The cults' websites are the same. They never mention their founders' false prophecies, legal troubles, polygamy, etc. I understand why they leave those things off their websites. They're embarrassing! Putting that kind of information on display would greatly injure their ability to attract new followers.

Knowing all of this, is what makes this seventh line of evidence—the Bible's forthrightness about its authors' and characters' failures—so remarkable.

Over and over, the authors of the Bible avoid the temptation to cast themselves, the fathers of the faith (e.g., Abraham or Moses), or their own people (the Israelites) in good light. From beginning to end, the Biblical writers are very open and forthright about their failures, weaknesses, downfalls, and sins.

Of course, this doesn't prove that what they wrote in the Bible is true, but I think it helps strengthen the case that the Bible appears to be an honest work. Allow me to remind you of some things we read about in the Bible:

- Noah's drunkenness and inappropriate nakedness shortly after the Flood (Genesis 9:21–22)

- Abraham's lying (on more than one occasion) about Sarah being his sister (Genesis 12:13, 20:2)
- Moses's murder of a man in Egypt (Exodus 2:11–12), his outburst of anger in the wilderness, how he misrepresented God and as a result wasn't allowed to enter the Promised Land (Numbers 20:10–12)

Who wrote the books of Exodus and Numbers where these matters are explained? Moses. He tells us about his failures in his own writings. These sound like the words of someone who was committed to communicating the truth. We read of:

- The nation of Israel rejecting God on numerous occasions to worship false gods—e.g., in the Book of Judges

Who gave us the Scriptures? The Jews. Would they include this in their history if it were not true?

- David's adulterous relationship with Bathsheba and subsequent murder of her husband Uriah (2 Samuel 11)
- Solomon's out of control sinful adultery and polygamy (1 Kings 11:1–3)
- Jesus rebuking the disciples on the sinking boat for being men "of little faith" (Matthew 8:26)
- Jesus calling Peter "Satan" (Mark 8:33)
- The disciples' arguments over which one of them was greatest, followed by Jesus's correction (Luke 9:46, 22:24)
- Peter denying he knew Jesus, after promising he would

never do such a thing (Matthew 26:72)
- The disciples falling asleep when Jesus asked them to pray (Mark 14:32–41)
- Peter cutting off the ear of the priest's servant, swiftly drawing a rebuke from Jesus (John 18:10)
- The disciples running away to save their own lives when Jesus was arrested (Mark 14:50)
- Paul's confession that he was "a wretched man" (Romans 7:24) and the "chief" of sinners (1 Timothy 1:15)
- Peter's fear of being seen eating with Gentiles (Galatians 2:11–12)
- Paul and Barnabas's argument over Mark being allowed to travel with them (Acts 15:37–39)
- John being rebuked by an angel after falling at his feet to worship him—twice! (Revelation 19:10, 22:8–9)

Friend, this is just a small sampling. Would the Biblical writers make these things up? I have a hard time believing that. The fact that the authors of the Bible include these details throughout the Old and New Testaments suggests these men were more interested in telling the truth than making themselves look good.

If you were inventing a religion or an account of how God has intervened in history, would you make up and include these kinds of details about yourself? I wouldn't. And there's something else I wouldn't do. I wouldn't risk dying a painful death seeking to convince people my lie was true. And that brings up an eighth line of evidence for the Bible's reliability.

Evidence No. 8
THE PERSECUTION ENDURED BY THE EARLY CHRISTIANS
Slain for Their Story

It is an accepted historical fact that the Christian faith (a religion built upon the preaching of the resurrection of its leader) originated in approximately AD 32 right in the very city of Jerusalem where Jesus had been publicly crucified and buried.[152] This in itself is a good piece of evidence that Jesus's resurrection actually occurred. Why? Because a message calling people to repent and put their faith in a risen man could never have gained any substantial following in Jerusalem if the tomb had not actually been empty and had people not seen Jesus alive after His crucifixion.

The message of a risen man could not have been maintained a moment in Jerusalem if the grave was still occupied. Remember, Jesus's disciples didn't run off to Athens or Rome to preach that Jesus was risen from the dead (where the facts could not be verified). They went right back to the city of Jerusalem where they would have been quickly exposed and disproved—if what

....

152. See "Christianity," *The Encyclopedia Britannica* (2013), http://www.britannica.com/EBchecked/topic/115240/Christianity.

they were teaching was false.[153] The critics could have exposed the disciples as liars and Christianity would never have gotten off the ground. The Pharisees or the Roman soldiers could have said, "Hey! Here is the body!" and squashed the whole movement. But that never happened! And not only did Christianity originate there in Jerusalem, it thrived there.

Luke, whose writings have been confirmed by numerous historical investigations and archaeological discoveries,[154] tells us 3000 people believed the first post-resurrection sermon preached a few minutes' walk from the tomb (Acts 2:41). Later, in the same chapter, Luke says the church was growing daily (Acts 2:47). By Acts 4:4, Luke declares there were 5000 believers comprising the early Christian church in Jerusalem. By Acts 6:7, Luke just says the number of disciples "continued to increase greatly *in Jerusalem*," apparently losing count!

And not only did Christianity flourish in Jerusalem, it went on to triumph over a number of competing ideologies and eventually overwhelm the entire Roman Empire. By the early fourth century, when the Roman Emperor Constantine converted to Christianity, historians say there were around thirty million Christians![155] And all of this happened in spite of the fact that the earliest Christians faced intense persecution.

Luke, who records the phenomenal growth of the church, tells us in the Book of Acts that this happened even as believers were threatened (4:18), imprisoned (12:4, 16:23, 24:27), beaten

....

153. Josh McDowell, *A Ready Defense* (1993), 232.

154. I discuss this in more detail in *Archaeological Evidence for the Bible* (2012), 127f.

155. Rodney Stark, *The Triumph of Christianity* (2011), 156.

(16:22), stoned to death (7:58, 14:19), killed with the sword (12:2), and had their homes attacked by angry mobs (17:5). But this kind of treatment has been confirmed *outside* of the Bible as well.

Flavius Josephus, Eusebius, Tertullian, and other independent extrabiblical sources[156] record for us that many of Jesus's earliest followers, including the apostles, suffered intense persecution and even death for their on-going belief and preaching that Jesus was Lord and was risen from the dead. We are told in these extrabiblical sources:

- Matthew was slain with an axe in Ethiopia
- Mark died in Alexandria, in northern Egypt, after having been cruelly dragged through the streets of that city
- Luke was hung to death in Greece
- John was tortured and then banished to the island of Patmos in the Mediterranean Sea (Revelation 1:9)
- James, the brother of John, was beheaded in Jerusalem (Acts 12:2)
- James the Less (Mark 15:40) was thrown down from a temple structure and then stoned and beaten
- Philip was hung up against a pillar in Heiropolis and stoned to death
- Bartholomew was flayed alive
- Andrew was bound to a cross and left to die

156. Hegesippus, Polycarp, Ignatius, Cornelius Tacitus, Dionysius, Clement of Alexandria, Clement of Rome, Origen. For a good overview of these sources and what they said regarding this matter, see Gary Habermas and Michael Licona, *The Case for the Resurrection of Jesus* (2004), 56–62.

- Jude was shot to death with arrows
- Matthias (the apostle chosen to replace Judas) was first stoned, then beheaded
- Barnabas was stoned to death
- Paul, after being stoned, imprisoned, beat with rods, and flogged with whips (2 Corinthians 11:23–28), was finally beheaded in Rome
- Thomas was speared to death in southeast India
- Peter was crucified upside down in Rome

That's sobering to think of. Question. Were these men lying? I find it very difficult to believe these men "made up a story" about Jesus and then spent years enduring persecution, imprisonments, and such, only to die these kinds of painful deaths. As I pointed out in chapter one, deceivers lie to *get out* of trouble or gain some type of advantage or benefit. What these men said about Jesus resulted in rejection, persecution, torture, and martyrdom.

Of course, there are people who are willing to die today for something they *think* or *hope* is true. Muslim terrorists come to mind. But nobody willingly dies for something they *know* is a lie. And Jesus's disciples were at a unique place in history. They lived in and around Jerusalem in the first century where Jesus was publicly crucified and buried in a tomb. So they were in a place historically to *know for certain* whether or not they had seen Jesus alive after His crucifixion or not.

Muslim terrorists today are not in such a place. They die for something they *think* is true, something they *hope* is true. But if they lived back in the seventh century at the time of Muhammad and knew for certain he was not a prophet of God, he never performed any miracles, and there weren't 72 virgins waiting for them in Heaven, they would not strap on explosives and blow themselves (and innocent bystanders) up. Nobody willingly dies for something they *know* is a lie.

And yet, Jesus's disciples, all the way back in the first century, sealed their testimonies with their own blood, claiming all the way to the end that the long-awaited Messiah and Savior of the world lived among them, became a sacrifice for our sins, and rose from the dead. That, to me, is persuasive evidence these men were telling the truth about Jesus.

For more on the persecution the early Christians faced, I recommend:

- Eusebius, *Ecclesiastical History*
- Tacitus, *Annals*, Book XV
- John Fox, *Fox's Book of Martyrs*
- Rodney Stark, *The Triumph of Christianity* (2011), especially "Persecution and Commitment," 137–152

Evidence No. 9
THE TESTIMONY OF THE SON OF GOD

Scripture in the Sight of Jesus

The compelling evidence that Jesus actually lived, fulfilled hundreds of Old Testament prophecies, and rose from the dead[157] has led myself and millions of people down through the ages to conclude Jesus is the Son of God—just as He claimed (John 3:18). Well, if there's anyone we can trust regarding the Scriptures and whether or not they are the Word of God, it's the One who proved Himself to be the Son of God. And Jesus assured us the Jewish Scriptures (as they existed in His time) could be trusted. For example, Jesus taught that the Scriptures were:

A. Without Error

He summarized the entirety of God's Word with one word in His prayer to His Father: "Thy word is *truth*" (John 17:17).

B. Historically Reliable

Jesus affirmed as historically true numerous passages in the Old

---

157. I lay out some of the evidence for the resurrection in my DVD "The Case for the Resurrection." We also have many articles and books on this at AlwaysBeReady.com. Click on "Resurrection of Christ."

Testament, including:

- The account of Adam and Eve as the first married couple (Mark 10:3–9)
- Cain's murder of Abel (Luke 11:51)
- The destruction of the world by a flood in the days of Noah (Matthew 24:37–39)
- The existence of Abraham, Isaac, Jacob, David, Solomon, Daniel, Isaiah, Elijah, Zechariah (e.g., Matthew 8:11, 12:3, 42, 23:35)
- The supernatural destruction of Sodom and Gomorrah (Luke 17:28–29)
- Moses's encounter with God at the burning bush (Luke 20:37–38)
- Moses lifting up the bronze serpent in the wilderness (John 3:14)
- Moses's authorship of the Torah—the first five books of the Old Testament (John 5:46–47; Luke 24:27)
- The manna in the wilderness that fed the Israelites (John 6:32–33, 49)
- The drought and famine during the days of Elijah (Luke 4:25–27)
- The account of Jonah in the great fish (Matthew 12:40)
- The Ninevites' repentance (Matthew 12:41)

Jesus's references to these incidents showed His total confidence in their factual historicity. He did not merely *allude* to these stories, He *authenticated* them as being completely trustworthy.[158]

C. Divinely Authoritative

When Jesus was in the wilderness being tempted by Satan (Matthew 4:1–11), He resisted this ungodly foe by quoting Scripture. Over and over again, Jesus responded to Satan and His other critics (the Pharisees, Sadducees, scribes) by pointing to Scripture, saying: "It is written" or "Have you not read?" (Matthew 4:4–10, 19:4, 21:13; Mark 7:6). He did the same with His disciples (Matthew 26:31; Mark 14:21; Luke 24:46). Why? Because He believed Scripture is authoritative on all matters related to faith and practice.

D. Accurate Regarding Human Origins

When it comes to the whole debate today over evolution versus creation, Jesus affirmed the early chapters of Genesis were accurate when He said, "Have you not read, that He who created them from the beginning made them male and female" (Matthew 19:4). Adam and Eve didn't come on the scene after billions of years of mutations and evolution. No. God created them all the way back in the *beginning*—just like Moses reported in the Book of Genesis.

E. Infallible (Dependable or Unbreakable)

Jesus assured His critics, "The Scripture cannot be broken" (John 10:35). In other words, what God has declared in the Scriptures *will* come to pass. The Scriptures are not going to break down on

158. Charles Ryrie, *Basic Theology* (1999), 98–99.

their way to being fulfilled.

F. Indestructible

In His Sermon on the Mount, Jesus proclaimed, "Until heaven and earth pass away, not the smallest letter or stroke shall pass away from the Law, until all is accomplished" (Matthew 5:18).

Friend, if Jesus was a prophet of God—as even the Quran teaches[159]—or a "good teacher" (as so many are willing to believe) it would be wise for us to take His word on the matter—*the Bible is a historically reliable, divinely authoritative, dependable, error free, indestructible book.*

SKEPTIC: "Come on, Charlie. You're referring to the words of Jesus *in* the Bible to help prove the Bible. That's circular reasoning."

It isn't. As I pointed out earlier, the Bible is not a single book. It is a collection of 66 books written by numerous authors. So, to quote Jesus's words recorded by Matthew, Mark, Luke, or John to help shed light on the reliability of something Moses or another author wrote in a different book is not circular reasoning at all. I am quoting independent sources. We've bound these sources together but they *are* independent sources.

SKEPTIC: "Okay, but Jesus only said those things about the Old Testament writings. The New Testament had not yet been written."

You're right. Jesus *did* say those things about the Old Testament (as I noted at the beginning of the chapter). But He also

---

159. Quran 4:171.

promised His disciples God's aid (the Holy Spirit) to write the New Testament. On the eve of His crucifixion, Jesus told them, "The Helper, the Holy Spirit, whom the Father will send in My name, He will teach you all things, and bring to your remembrance all things that I said to you" (John 14:26). A short time later, that same evening, Jesus told His disciples, "When He, the Spirit of truth, comes, He will guide you into all the truth; for He will not speak on His own initiative, but whatever He hears, He will speak; and He will disclose to you what is to come" (John 16:13).

As these men went out into the world to tell people about Jesus (Matthew 28:18–20), whether by preaching and teaching, or penning the gospels and epistles, they were going to have the supernatural guidance of the Holy Spirit to guide them. Jesus assured them of that.

So, Jesus *validated* the trustworthiness of the Old Testament and He *pre-authenticated* the trustworthiness of the New Testament. Based on Jesus's testimony, you can trust both.

Remember the previous four evidences:

M.A.P.S.

<u>M</u> = Manuscript Evidence

<u>A</u> = Authors' Forthrightness About Failures

<u>P</u> = Persecution Endured By The Early Christians

<u>S</u> = Son of God's View of Scripture

Evidence No. 10
THE BIBLE'S TRANSFORMING POWER FOR GOOD

Scripture's Sway Over Hearts

Muhammad, the founder of Islam, was born in Mecca in AD 570. What Muhammad's followers did after his death in 632 still causes historians to shudder. By 638, Muhammad's followers seized the Holy Land by force.[160] Within ten years of Muhammad's death, soldiers of Islam (Islam's first missionaries) conquered Iraq, Syria, Persia, and Egypt.[161] Within the course of that first century, they spread the Islamic Empire into Central Asia, India, China, across North Africa, and all the way to the shores of the Atlantic Ocean in Southern France and Spain.[162]

Were it not for Charles Martel in 732 at a battle in Tours, France, millions more today might be speaking Arabic and kneeling toward Mecca five times a day to pray. It was there in France, that Martel (a ruler of the Franks) defeated the advancing Muslim armies and ended their advance into Europe. Many

160. By "Holy Land," I'm referring to Israel, popularly known as Palestine.

161. John L. Esposito, *Islam: The Straight Path* (1998), 33; Rodney Stark, *The Triumph of Christianity* (2011), 200–204.

162. George W. Braswell, *Islam: Its Prophet, Peoples, Politics and Power* (1996), 25–26.

historians believe that if it were not for that successful battle, all of Europe may have fallen to Islam.[163]

So, Islam spread far and wide as it was forced upon tens of millions by military conquest (*jihad*). It is an undeniable fact of history that Islam spread by the sword.[164] Sadly, this was carried out in obedience to Muhammad's teachings.[165]

Now, contrast the spread of Islam with the spread of Christianity. The latter spread over the first three centuries through the simple preaching of Jesus's life-changing teachings. As I discussed in chapter eight, it was the *Christians* who were being put to death. But in light of all God had done for them, it was a price many early Christians were willing to pay to remain faithful to Jesus and ensure others heard the good news of His death and resurrection. And so, they took the gospel and the teachings of Jesus—the teachings of the Bible—from Jerusalem to the far ends of the Roman Empire and beyond. And millions believed. As I noted previously, there were around thirty million Chris-

....

163. "Battle of Tours," *The Encyclopedia Britannica* (2013), http://www.britannica.com/EBchecked/topic/600883/Battle-of-Tours.

164. This is something widely acknowledged by historians. See "Islam" in *The Encyclopedia Britannica* (2013). Note the place where it says pagans numbering in the millions "were required to either accept Islam or die." http://www.britannica.com/EBchecked/topic/295507/Islam.

165. Muhammad said, "Make war on them until idolatry shall cease and God's religion shall reign supreme" (Quran 8:39). Elsewhere in the Quran he said, "So when the sacred months have passed away, then slay the idolaters wherever you find them, and take them captives and besiege them and lie in wait for them in every ambush, then if they repent and keep up prayer and pay the poor-rate [a burdensome tax imposed on non Muslims], leave their way free to them...Fight those who believe not in Allah nor the Last Day... even if they are of the People of the Book [the Bible, i.e., Jews and Christians], until they pay the tax and they are in a state of subjection" (Quran 9:5, 29). In his farewell address in March 632, Muhammad said, "I was ordered to fight all men until they say 'There is no god but Allah.'" Quoted in Efraim Karsh, *Islamic Imperialism: A History* (2007), 4.

tians in the Roman Empire shortly after Constantine issued his "Edict of Milan" ending persecution of Christians in AD 313.[166]

People in far away cities like Corinth, Ephesus, Philippi, Rome, Colossae, and Thessalonica had heard the Word of God and "accepted it not as the word of men, but for what it really is, the word of God" (1 Thessalonians 2:13). As a result, they "turned to God from idols to serve a living and true God" (1 Thessalonians 1:9) revealed in Jesus. And though many of them had been involved in a variety of sins (fornication, adultery, homosexuality, drunkenness, thievery—see 1 Corinthians 6:9–10), they turned away from these sins. They had the power to leave these sins behind because as Paul said, "the word of God... performs its work in you who believe" (1 Thessalonians 2:13). The Spirit of God working through the Word of God (Ephesians 6:17) changed millions of lives in the Roman Empire.

And God's Word continues to change lives today. Wherever the Bible has gone and been received—from prisons to remote villages deep inside third world countries—it has had a transforming effect on peoples' lives for good. Countless people (including myself!) who would testify that they were immoral, godless sinners, drowning in a cesspool of sins (harmful to themselves and others), have been transformed into men and women who reflect Jesus as they have prayerfully read the Bible. Dr. John MacArthur points out:

---

166. Rodney Stark says, "It is generally agreed that by the year 350, Christians were in the majority—if barely—amounting to somewhat more than 30 million who were at least nominal Christians." *The Triumph of Christianity*, 156.

Millions of people—from great heads of state to brilliant educators and scientists, from philosophers and writers to generals and historians—could all testify about how the Bible has changed their lives. As somebody has said, "A Bible that is falling apart usually belongs to somebody who isn't." Millions of people are living proof that the Bible can put lives together and keep them that way.[167]

In addition to introducing people to the true and living God and the forgiveness and "everlasting life" (John 3:16) He makes available to them, the Bible's words have inspired people to:

- Build countless hospitals, refugee camps, and orphanages
- Start thousands of schools, including many of the world's greatest universities; e.g., Harvard, Yale, Princeton, Oxford, and Cambridge were all started by Christians for Christian purposes[168]
- Work for the equality of people with different skin colors; e.g., Martin Luther King, Jr. was a Christian pastor of a Baptist church
- Investigate the world and universe scientifically; e.g., many of the great early pioneers in science claimed it was their Christian worldview that provided the motivation to study the world of nature and take science to new

167. John MacArthur, *Why Believe the Bible* (2007), 25.

168. Alvin Schmidt, *How Christianity Changed the World* (2004), 190–191. For more on this, see Schmidt's "Christianity's Imprint on Education," 170–193.

heights;[169] Copernicus, Kepler, Galileo, Bacon, Pascal, Newton, Boyle, Mendel, Faraday, Pasteur were Christians or at least had high views of the Bible[170]

- Create beautiful paintings, statues, carvings, and architectural works, e.g., Rembrandt's art, Michelangelo's paintings in the Sistine Chapel, Leonardo's *Last Supper*, European cathedrals[171]

- Further the development of beautiful music; Bach, Handel, Mozart, Vivaldi, Mendelssohn, Stravinsky, and Vaughan Williams were inspired by Jesus's life, death and resurrection[172]

- Write great literature; Shakespeare's writings contain hundreds of quotes from the Bible; C. S. Lewis and J. R. R. Tolkien were Christians[173]

- Abolish slavery, e.g., William Wilberforce and Abraham Lincoln were both Christians[174]

....

169. Ibid., 218–247. For more on science and its early Christian connections, see John Lennox, *God's Undertaker: Has Science Buried God?* (2009), 9–10, 20–30; Rodney Stark, *The Triumph of Christianity* (2011), 284–292; Dinesh D'Souza, *What's So Great About Christianity?* (2007), 91–111.

170. For more on great scientists who were Christians, see Dr. Henry F. Schaefer, "Scientists and Their Gods: Science and Christianity: Conflict or Coherence?" http://bib.irr.org/scientists-and-their-gods. Also see Henry Morris, *Men of Science, Men of God: Great Scientists Who Believed the Bible* (1982).

171. For more, see Alvin Schmidt, *How Christianity Changed the World* (2004), 292–313.

172. Alvin Schmidt, *How Christianity Changed the World* (2004), 342. For more, see 314–344.

173. For more, see "The Bible and Literature" in D. James Kennedy and Jerry Newcombe, *What if the Bible Had Never Been Written?* (1998), 119–145.

174. For more on the topic of slavery in the Bible, see Vincent Carroll and David Shiflett, *Christianity on Trial* (2002), 24–53; Alvin Schmidt, *How Christianity Changed the World* (2004), 272–291; "Bible Difficulties" at AlwaysBeReady.com.

- Treat women better; New Testament teachings such as "Husbands, love your wives, just as Christ also loved the church and gave Himself up for her" (Ephesians 5:25) helped to raise women's dignity, freedom, and rights to a level previously unknown in any culture

Where else do women have more freedom, opportunity, and human worth than in countries that have been highly influenced by the Christian ethic?[175]

- Love, cherish, and remain faithful to their spouses[176]
- Consider it more blessed to give than to receive (Acts 20:35)
- Love and care for lonely, needy, and fatherless children (Psalm 68:6; James 1:27); e.g., Christians working alongside Samaritan's Purse Ministry have given away more than 100 million (1993–2013) shoeboxes filled with toys, clothes, and toiletries at Christmas to less fortunate children all over the world[177]
- Look after widows (Exodus 22:22–23; 1 Timothy 5:3–16)
- Love and treat their neighbors as they would desire to be treated (Matthew 22:39)

....

175. Alvin Schmidt, *How Christianity Changed the World* (2004), 122. For more on this, see Schmidt's chapter "Women Receive Freedom and Dignity," 97–124.

176. Bradford Wilcox, a leading sociologist at the University of Virginia and Director of the National Marriage Project, found in 2007 that active, conservative members of Protestant churches are 35 percent less likely to divorce than Americans who are religiously unaffiliated. See http://www.breakpoint.org/bpcommentaries/entry/13/20460?tmpl=-component&print=1.

177. See http://www.samaritanspurse.org/what-we-do/operation-christmas-child.

- Feed the hungry, volunteer at homeless shelters (Psalm 82:3)
- Do unto others as they would have done to them (Matthew 7:12)

The Bible has truly made the world a better place. If you doubt this, perhaps the following scenario will help change your mind.

Let's imagine your car breaks down late one night somewhere in a bad part of town. You're stranded on a lonely dark street and much to your disappointment your phone battery has just reached empty. You get out of your car wondering what you're going to do only to see ten big burly men coming out of a house and walking toward you. Would it be comforting to know they were just coming out of a Bible study? Surely it would be a comfort![178] And that's because most of us know from experience that those who prayerfully study the Bible typically live lives that have been changed for good—their own good and that of their fellow man.

The historian Philip Schaff summarized the enormous impact the Bible has had on people when he wrote this about Jesus and His words:

Jesus of Nazareth, without money and arms, conquered more millions than Alexander, Caesar, Muhammad, and

----

178. I've adapted this scenario (with some changes) originally told by Dennis Praeger, then retold by Ravi Zacharias, and cited in Kennedy and Newcombe, *What if the Bible Had Never Been Written?* (1998), 220.

Napoleon; without science and learning, He shed more light on things human and divine than all philosophers and scholars combined; without the eloquence of schools, He spoke such words of life as were never spoken before or since, and produced effects which lie beyond the reach of orator or poet; without writing a single line, He set more pens in motion, and furnished themes for more sermons, orations, discussions, learned volumes, works of art, and songs of praise than the whole army of great men of ancient and modern times.[179]

No other book in the world has had the far-reaching, culture-crossing, multi-generational transforming effect on human lives and societies for good, the Bible has.[180] And the reason the Bible has had such a unique, profound effect on human hearts is because it is "the word of God" (Ephesians 6:17). God blesses and transforms the lives of those who receive it and prayerfully ponder what it has to say with the intent to obey (Psalm 19:7; 1 Thessalonians 2:13; Hebrews 4:12).

SKEPTIC: "Well, you talk about this ignoring the fact that the Bible has inspired a lot of awful things like the killing of thousands of women during the Salem witch hunts and even more during the Spanish Inquisition. You said earlier that

---

179. Philip Schaff, *The Person of Christ* (1866), 48.

180. If you would like to read more about how the Bible has changed the world for good, I highly recommend the book *What if the Bible Had Never Been Written?* by D. James Kennedy and Jerry Newcombe. It is excellent. Also good, are *How Christianity Changed the World* by Alvin Schmidt and *Christianity on Trial* by Vincent Carroll and David Shiflett.

Christianity spread through the preaching of the gospel. What about the Crusades? Christians are guilty of using violence to spread their message!"

Well in response to this, yes, people claiming to be Christians have unfortunately have done some awful things. And that is deeply grieving. But I think it's important to point out that when they did these things, they were not acting in a Christian manner. Jesus said:

> But I say to you who hear, love your enemies, do good to those who hate you, bless those who curse you, pray for those who mistreat you. Whoever hits you on the cheek, offer him the other also; and whoever takes away your coat, do not withhold your shirt from him either. Give to everyone who asks of you, and whoever takes away what is yours, do not demand it back. Treat others the same way you want them to treat you (Luke 6:27–31).

Surely the things that occurred during the Salem witch trials in 1692 were not a fulfillment of Jesus's words. But I think it's important to note that the trials did not result in the deaths of thousands—as is sometimes thrown around in poorly researched articles on the Internet. The trials resulted in the deaths of nineteen people.[181] I'm not seeking to make light of those deaths. I just want to make sure we stick to the facts. Also worth pointing out is that it was Christians (particularly a

181. "Salem Witch Trials," *The Encyclopedia Britannica* (2013), http://www.britannica.com/EBchecked/topic/519064/Salem-witch-trials.

Puritan minister by the name of Increase Mather) who brought about an end to the trials. Mather spoke out powerfully against what was happening and they came to an end.[182] Critics bent on painting Christianity in as negative a light as possible never tell you *that* part of the story.

SKEPTIC: "Well, what about the Inquisitions? Thousands of people were burned at the stake by the Catholic Church!"

There are some things the Catholic Church did in the past that were awful—including killing Christians who disagreed with their teachings or who attempted to translate the Bible into modern languages the people could read.[183] So, yes, the Inquisitions are a dark and tragic chapter in the history of the Catholic Church. But this doesn't mean the Bible is unreliable. The Catholic Church acted *contrary* to the Bible. This is one of the reasons Christians broke away from the Catholic Church in the Reformation five hundred years ago.

Regarding the Crusades, I would note two things. First, the Crusades were not carried out to spread the Christian faith. The initial rationale for the Crusades—first launched in 1095, a thousand years after Jesus—was to take back the land Muslims had seized by military conquest from the Christians.[184] *The Encyclopedia Britannica* confirms that the Crusades:

....

182. Dr. John Woodbridge, interview with Lee Strobel in *The Case for Faith* (2000), 210.

183. I discuss some of these disagreements at AlwaysBeReady.com. Click on "Catholicism."

184. Norman Geisler and Frank Turek, *I Don't Have Enough Faith to Be an Atheist* (2004), 296. For more on this, see Rodney Stark, *God's Battalions: The Case for the Crusades.*

[W]ere organized in response to centuries of Muslim wars of expansion. Their objectives were to check the spread of Islam, to retake control of the Holy Land...Approximately two-thirds of the ancient Christian world had been conquered by Muslims by the end of the 11th century, including the important regions of Palestine, Syria, Egypt, and Anatolia.[185]

The destruction and threat to sacred places in Jerusalem,[186] the murder, torture, enslavement, robbery, and harassment of Christian pilgrims traveling to the Holy Land all served to provoke the Crusades.[187] So, that is important to note. The Crusades were not launched to spread the gospel or force Christianity upon Muslims.[188]

Second, I would remind the reader that any evil committed during the Crusades—and there were atrocities[189]—*contradicted* the teachings of the Bible. At His arrest in the Garden of Gethsemane, Jesus rebuked Peter for striking a man with his sword, saying, "Put your sword back into its place; for all those who take up the sword shall perish by the sword" (Matthew 26:52).

---

185. "Crusades," *The Encyclopedia Britannica* (2013), http://www.britannica.com/EB-checked/topic/144695/Crusades.

186. For example, in 1009 Muslims destroyed the Church of the Holy Sepulcher in Jerusalem—even the tomb itself, leaving only traces of the hollow in the rocks.

187. Rodney Stark, *The Triumph of Christianity* (2011), 217.

188. Rodney Stark says, "The crusaders made no attempt to impose Christianity on the Muslims. In fact, Muslims who lived in crusader-won territories were generally allowed to retain their property and livelihood, and always their religion." *The Triumph of Christianity*, 228.

189. See Bruce Shelley, *Church History in Plain Language* (1995), 188.

At His interrogation before Pontius Pilate, Jesus said, "My kingdom is not of this world. If My kingdom were of this world, then My servants would be fighting" (John 18:36). Jesus's teachings were never to be furthered with violence.

Of course, this doesn't mean Christians cannot fight in certain just causes as part of their country's military. Christians have long understood there are Biblically defensible principles for a "just war."[190] Unfortunately, some of these principles were thrown to the wind during the Crusades. But again, these kinds of behaviors (then and now) *contradict* the teachings of the Bible.

SKEPTIC: "But what about the Old Testament, when Joshua and the nation of Israel were instructed by God to go through the land of Canaan and kill everyone? How could a loving God command something like that?"

As we consider God's judgment on the Canaanites (or Sodom, Gomorrah, or Israel later on for that matter) it's good to remember a few important facts.

1. God is sovereign over life (Deuteronomy 32:39; Job 1:21). He created humanity and He has the right to do whatever He deems best with His creation. All life belongs to Him. If He

---

190. Albert Mohler summarizes them: "The Just War tradition insists that war must be the last resort, after all reasonable alternatives have failed. A lawful authority must authorize the military action, and that authority must be driven by an intention to establish a righteous peace—not to gain territory or claim the goods of another lawful nation. Furthermore, any military action must be proportionate to the good that can be gained. No military action is justified that is not absolutely required. There must also be a very real hope of success. In the final analysis, the only justifiable war is defensive rather than offensive—it is undertaken to right a wrong, not to gain an advantage. Once military action is necessary and justified, commanders must take care to protect civilians to the greatest extent possible..." Source: "Is War Ever Justified? A Reality Check," http://www.albertmohler.com/2004/04/19/is-war-ever-justified-a-reality-check.

regards a group of people wicked enough to deserve judgment, then He has that prerogative.

Many people believe the Allied Powers in World War II had a moral obligation, even a God-given obligation, to go to war against the Nazis in order to end the great evils they were committing. If human governments have the right to send in a military force to put an end to evil doers, does God not have the same right? Surely He does. I wonder how many critics of the Bible might have actually supported the war effort if they had lived at the time of Joshua and were aware of the great atrocities going on in Canaan?

2. The Canaanites were guilty of terrible evils. Leviticus 18, Deuteronomy 18:9–14, and elsewhere, tell us the Canaanites at the time of Joshua were an exceedingly wicked people who were indulging in incest, adultery, polygamy, bestiality, homosexuality, witchcraft, child sacrifice to a deity named Molech, and a variety of other "abominable customs" (Leviticus 18:30).[191] The Canaanites had become a dangerous threat to their posterity, neighbors, and the Israelites. So, God—who has every right to intervene in the affairs of the world *He* made—determined the Canaanites' time in His land, on His planet, was up.

3. God is merciful and slow to anger (Genesis 15:16; Numbers 14:18). He does not delight in the death of the wicked; He would rather people turn from their wicked ways and live lives He can bless (Ezekiel 18:23). If the Canaanites had turned their backs on their evil ways as the Ninevites did (Jonah 3:10), I'm certain

....

191. I discuss the archaeological evidence for child-sacrifice in my book *Archaeological Evidence for the Bible* (2012), 66–68.

God would have shown them mercy (see Genesis 18:32). But they did not repent. So, God's judgment fell on them. God used the Israelites to drive them out of the land—just as He would use the Assyrians and Babylonians centuries later to drive the Israelites out of the land for the same sins!

4. The instructions God gave the Israelites (Deuteronomy 20:16–18) were entirely situation-specific. That is, they were given to a particular nation for a particular situation. God's instructions to the Israelites were not open-ended; they weren't given to allow the Jews (or anyone for that matter) the freedom to attack whomever they pleased. And Jews and Christians have long known this. How often do you see them blowing up innocent people as they scream out verses from the Book of Deuteronomy or Joshua? Exactly.

The critic of the Bible who brings up the Book of Joshua (or the persecution of witches, the Inquisition, etc.) and thinks, "I would never believe in God—the Bible has inspired so much harm throughout history!" should bear in mind that far more harm has been unleashed on the world by men under the influence of secular and atheistic philosophies than by erring Christians, Jews, or Popes.[192] Think of the 66 million people put to death under Lenin, Stalin, and Khrushchev, the 26 million people under Mao Zedong between 1949 and 1965, another two million under Pol Pot.[193] In their excellent book *Christianity on*

----

192. Dr. John Lennox of Oxford University discusses this in his book *Gunning for God* (2011), 69, 83–95.

193. Greg Koukl, "The Real Murderers: Atheism or Christianity?" http://www.str.org/articles/the-real-murderers-atheism-or-christianity.

Trial: Arguments Against Anti-Religious Bigotry, Vincent Carroll and David Shiflett point out:

> The body count from the two great barbarisms of the twentieth century, Communism and Nazism, is extraordinary enough on its own. Communism's toll ran to perhaps 100 million: 65 million in China, 20 million in the Soviet Union, 2 million in Cambodia, 2 million in North Korea, 1 million in Eastern Europe and 10 million in various other spots around the globe.[194]

Atheistic and secular philosophies have a far bloodier track record than what's been done in the name of Christianity.

SKEPTIC: "I still don't think this tenth line of evidence (the Bible's transforming power for good) is very persuasive. Mormons could use the same argument in support of the Book of Mormon."

The Book of Mormon published in 1830 has certainly made an impact on the lives of certain people. Fourteen million Mormons in the world might testify to that.[195] But numerically, this is a minuscule drop in the bucket compared to the impact the Bible has had on the two *billion* Christians in the world, not to mention the millions of people who have been impacted by the Bible over the past two thousand years. And, in addition to that,

....

194. Vincent Carroll and David Shiflett, *Christianity on Trial* (2002), 109.

195. This is the number of members according to the Mormon Church as of December 2012. http://www.mormonnewsroom.org/article/2012-statistical-report-2013-april-general-conference.

it has been demonstrated in numerous ways that the Book of Mormon is an untrustworthy, deceptive work.[196] So, yes, it *has* had an impact on some people, but ultimately not a good one, for Joseph Smith's work is actually leading people *astray* from the truth about God.

Lastly, in response to the skeptic's objection, I would point out that this tenth line of evidence (the Bible's transforming power) is only a small part of my overall case. Taken alone, I agree, this evidence might be inconclusive. But, the case I've set forth in this concise book is a *cumulative* one. That is to say, I've been adding one line of evidence to another. When you consider all ten evidences together, they form what I believe is a compelling cumulative case for the Bible.

CONCLUSION

Friend, in light of...

- The hundreds of fulfilled prophecies
- Thousands of archaeological discoveries
- The Bible's internal consistency
- The extrabiblical historical confirmation
- The Bible's scientific accuracy and foresight
- Thousands of ancient handwritten manuscripts
- Thousands of quotations by the church fathers
- The authors' forthrightness about sin and failures

---

196. See the articles, books, and videos at AlwaysBeReady.com. Click on "Mormonism."

- The persecution endured by the early Christians
- The Bible's transforming power for good

I exhort you to trust the Bible. Read it with confidence. And read it often. What a blessing it is to know God and to prayerfully meditate on His Word every day as you allow Him to encourage you, teach you about Himself, give you wisdom for the decisions you're making, and transform your life.

If you've never placed your faith in Jesus Christ—do it today! There are no good reasons to wait. Two thousand years ago Jesus—God in the flesh—out of His great love for you, died on that cruel wooden Roman cross. Why? To take the punishment for your sins so you could be forgiven, rescued from spending eternity in Hell, and be brought back into a relationship with Him. He rose from the grave three days later and today He is offering mankind—you!—the "free gift" (Romans 6:23) of salvation and "everlasting life" (John 3:16) to all who will turn from their sins and place their faith in Him.

I encourage you to do that right now if you never have. A day of judgment *is* coming. You can stand before God still in your sins where you will be justly condemned and cast into Hell (Revelation 20) or you can stand before Him forgiven and welcomed into Paradise to enjoy everlasting life with God, the angels, and all the redeemed. The choice is yours.

**What will *you* do with God's offer
of reconciliation?**

Friend, I urge you, place your faith in Jesus. Talk to Him right now in prayer. Confess to Him that you are a sinner. Tell Him you want to turn from your sins and place your faith in Jesus as Lord and Savior. Ask Him to forgive you. Ask Him to change you and to fill you with the power of the Holy Spirit to live a life that is pleasing to Him. God bless you.

QUESTIONS
For Discussion

1. How strong of a case for the trustworthiness of the Bible do you think these ten lines of evidence build?

2. If you are still not convinced the Bible is trustworthy, what kind of evidence do you think it will take to change your mind? Could the reason you continue to reject the Bible be that you just don't want to submit your life to God?

3. What two or three evidences did you find most interesting? Why?

4. Which of the ten lines of evidence do you think might be most persuasive if you were to share it with your skeptical friends or family?

5. What evidence(s) would you like to learn more about?

6. Has the Bible changed your life? Do you think the change in your life is evidence for the reliability of the Bible? Why or why not?

7. If you believe the Bible is trustworthy, how should that affect your daily life? How should it affect opportunities you have to share with nonbelievers?

8. If you had one or two minutes to tell someone why you believe the Bible is trustworthy, what would you say?

INDEX

Qumran, Israel, where the Dead Sea Scrolls were discovered.

CHARLIE H. CAMPBELL

Charlie Campbell is the Director of the Always Be Ready Apologetics Ministry, an ordained pastor, author, and a popular guest teacher at churches around North America, speaking regularly on a wide variety of issues related to the defense of the Christian faith. His books and DVDs are used in churches around the world and have been endorsed by Charles Colson, Norman Geisler, Chuck Smith, Ed Hindson and Nancy Leigh DeMoss among others. Previously, he taught at the Calvary Chapel Bible College in Murrieta, California, and served as the Director of the School of Ministry at Calvary Chapel in Vista, California, where he taught courses on theology, apologetics, world religions, cults, eschatology, hermeneutics, homiletics and evangelism (1997–2006). Charlie resides in southern California with his wife and five children. You can find his resources at **AlwaysBeReady.com**

RELATED RESOURCES BY CHARLIE CAMPBELL
Available at AlwaysBeReady.com

EVIDENCE FOR THE EXISTENCE OF GOD (DVD)

Did the universe just pop into being from nothing and by nothing? Did the human body evolve into its present form by unguided natural causes? Seeking answers to questions like these led Charlie Campbell to abandon his atheism in 1990. In this 68 minute DVD Charlie Campbell shares some of the evidence from cosmology, biology, philosophy, history, and the Bible that changed his mind.

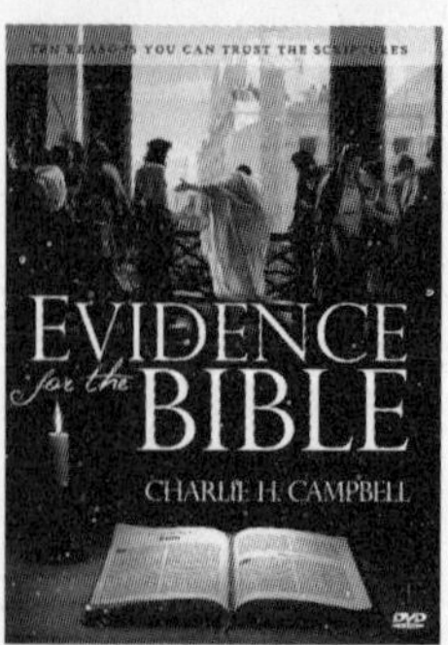

EVIDENCE FOR THE BIBLE (DVD)

Was the Bible written by deceitful men? Is the Bible out-of-sync with scientific discoveries? Has the Bible undergone corruption as it was translated down through the centuries? Are the persons, places and events mentioned in the Bible mythological? What sets the Bible apart from other religious writings like the Quran, Hindu Vedas, or Book of Mormon? Charlie Campbell answers those questions in this updated, expanded, third edition DVD. This DVD is an 83 minute visual presentation of content similar to what's in this book. If you enjoyed the content in this book and know someone you'd like to pass it on to who is not a reader, check out this DVD!

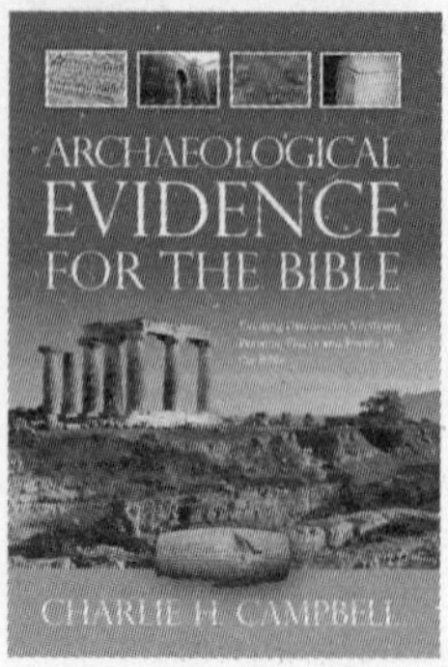

ARCHAEOLOGICAL EVIDENCE FOR THE BIBLE (BOOK)

For the past 150 years archaeologists have been verifying the exact truthfulness of the Bible's detailed records of various events, customs, persons, cities, nations, and geographical locations. In this book Charlie Campbell discusses dozens of fascinating discoveries—both old and new—that have overturned critics' attacks on the Bible and helped to confirm the historical reliability of the Scriptures. Full color paperback. 90 photographs. 150 pages.